THE ART OF HEALING LATINOS

The Art of Healing Latinos

Firsthand Accounts from Physicians and Other Health Advocates

Edited by

David E. Hayes-Bautista and Roberto Chiprut

Published for the UCLA Center for the
Study of Latino Health and Culture by the
UCLA Chicano Studies Research Center Press

Los Angeles 2008
Second Edition

Printed in the United States of America.

The opinions expressed in this book are those of the editors and authors and do
not necessarily reflect the opinions of AltaMed, California Hospital Medical Center,
Tower Health, or the Regents of the University of California.

Library of Congress Cataloging-in-Publication Data

The art of healing Latinos : firsthand accounts from physicians and other
health advocates / edited by David E. Hayes-Bautista and Roberto Chiprut.
--2nd ed.
    p. ; cm.
    Rev. ed. of: Healing Latinos / David Hayes-Bautista, Roberto Chiprut.
c1999.
    Includes bibliographical references and index.
    ISBN 978-0-89551-102-7 (pbk. : alk. paper)
    1. Hispanic Americans--Medical care--California. 2. Mexican Americans--Medical
care--California. 3. Transcultural medical care--California. 4. Physician and patient
--California. I.
Hayes-Bautista, David E., 1945- II. Chiprut, Roberto. III. Hayes-Bautista, David
E., 1945-
Healing Latinos. IV. University of California, Los Angeles. Center for the Study of
Latino Health.
    [DNLM: 1. Delivery of Health Care--United States--Personal
Narratives. 2.
Hispanic Americans--United States--Personal Narratives. 3. Cultural
Characteristics--United States--Personal Narratives. 4. Health
Behavior--ethnology--United States--Personal Narratives. 5.
Professional-Patient Relations--United States--Personal Narratives. WA
300
A784 2006]
    RA448.5.H57A78 2006
    362.1089'68073--dc22
                                        2007011933

 UCLA Chicano Studies Research Center
193 Haines Hall
Los Angeles, CA 90095-1544
www.chicano.ucla.edu

Director: Chon A. Noriega
Press Manager: Wendy Belcher
Production Editor: Rebecca Frazier
Business Manager: Lisa Liang
Production: William Morosi

Contents

In Memoriam: Roberto Chiprut

Roberto Salomon Chiprut Ovadía, MD, FACP, was a true *Chilango*, born and educated in Mexico City, to which he returned in 2000 to re-establish his practice. He received his medical education at the Universidad Nacional Autonoma de Mexico (UNAM), where he partook of a long tradition of medical education in the Americas that began in 1578, when the first chair of medicine was established at the Real y Pontificia Universidad de Mexico, the predecessor of UNAM. Chiprut did his training at the University of Tel Aviv, Baylor University, and the University of Miami.

After his training, Chiprut settled in Los Angeles. He established a private practice and was an attending internist and gastroenterologist at Cedars-Sinai Medical Center. An inveterate organizer, his concern for Latino patients with cancer led him to become involved in the founding of the support group Hermanos en la Lucha contra el Cancer, a part of the American Cancer Society. When the journal *Medicine of the Americas* was founded, he accepted an appointment as the international editor for Mexico. As a result of his research interests—which led to the authorship of more than fifty journal articles and three books—he took an appointment as clinical professor of medicine at the David Geffen School of Medicine at UCLA.

I had met him briefly at a number of events organized by the California Hispanic American Medical Association (CHAMA, one of the forerunners of today's California Latino Medical Association). One afternoon, he called me and asked if we could meet to discuss an important undertaking. He had been approached by a publisher of Spanish-language guides (*Tell-A-Maid, Tell-A-Gardener*) to develop a guide for medical personnel. He was not sure this was a good idea, and he asked me to come with him to the meeting with the publisher. So, my wife and I sat in on the meeting. Roberto was clearly against the idea of writing a simple phrase book, but seemed to have difficulty expressing why he found the notion so upsetting. Then, in the middle of the publisher's spiel, he suddenly blurted out, "This is all well and good if the doctor wants to tell the patient to sit down. But what if the patient wants to say something? What if the patient needs someone to talk to? This won't help at all." And he walked out of the meeting.

That evening, we talked over the events of the day. He was a little despondent, as he had wanted to write something to help his non-Latino colleagues better understand Latino patients. As we talked, it became clear that what he wanted to write was not simply a phrase book, but a book that would provide a deeper understanding of Latino patients and what makes them tick. He began to get excited again, and suddenly he blurted out (Roberto was a blurter), "We need to write a book that helps a physician get inside the mind of Latino patients, so that the healing process can begin as a mutual endeavor. We need to call the book *Healing Latinos*."

That was the genesis of this book. Events took Roberto away from us in 2002, but his influence continues. The first edition of *Healing Latinos: Realidad y Fantasía* sold out and has been unavailable for some time. As a tribute to our colleague and friend, we have undertaken a revision of that first edition, updating some chapters, to make this material and his vision available once again.

Roberto, we miss you, but, inspired by your example, we continue your work.

David E. Hayes-Bautista

Acknowledgments

*T*he editors are grateful to the seventeen collaborators, all based in Southern California, who agreed to contribute essays to this volume on their experiences of effective, culturally competent treatment of Latino patients. As physicians, researchers, authors, and activists in fields from pediatrics to geriatrics and oncology to psychology, most were Latino themselves and all had a majority of Latino patients. All were uniquely qualified to bridge the gap between the sophisticated world of American medicine and Latino culture. In their stories, which range from the coldly clinical to the emotionally moving, this group of dedicated caregivers show their devotion, care, and uncompromising skill. Our thanks go to them.

The preparation of this second edition of *Healing Latinos* was assisted by Jessica Iglesias, staff member of the UCLA Center for the Study of Latino Health and Culture, and Wendy Belcher, UCLA Chicano Studies Research Center. Maria Hayes-Bautista and our editor, Avril Angevine, worked on production for the first edition, which was published with the support of Cedars-Sinai Health System. Many thanks to all who contributed to both editions.

About the Authors

Roberto Chiprut

*F*or the Latino patient, cancer and death are frequently synonymous. Denial is frequent. As a result, Latinos have the highest rate of late diagnosis and advanced malignancy among cancer patients. **Dr. Jerome B. Block** ("The Meaning of Death"), an Anglo oncologist with an extraordinary interest in Latino culture, devoted a good portion of his life to improving the health and well-being of Latinos afflicted by cancer. As one of the most culturally competent non-Latino physicians in this country, Block understood the roles that religion, family, healers, and, most important of all, faith have in the healing process. His perspectives on weaving religion and spirituality into treatment, on the emotional commitment that Latino patients expect of their caregivers, and on the sensitive introduction of pain medications and advanced technologies into treatment were acquired through trial and error over his years of practice. By seeing Latinos at the moment of death, Block learned much about how his patients lived their lives. Block showed us that a practitioner can achieve high levels of cultural competence through sensitivity, respect, and patience. He attended Stanford University and received his MD from New York University, followed by training at Boston University and the University of Washington. In 1963 he served a year at the Weitzman Institute

in Rehovath, Israel. From 1974 Block was chief of the Division
of Medical Oncology and Hematology at the Harbor–UCLA
Medical Center in Torrance, California. He focused there on
teaching, patient care, and creating innovative programs in clinical research. He was previously director of the National Cancer
Institute's Baltimore Cancer Research Center, associate director
of the N.I.H. Clinical Center, and professor of medicine at UCLA.
He was the co-recipient of the Karger Memorial International
Prize for Leukemia Research and was honored by the Academia
Sinica of the Republic of China for developing Taiwan's first
training and certification programs in medical oncology from
1988 through 1991. After his semi-retirement, Block remained
a professor and maintained an active academic consultative practice, starting GSM (Genetic Services Management), an innovative
corporation for improving the quality of life of cancer patients. He
served most recently as the editor in chief of the journal *Medicine
of the Americas*, board member of the Harbor Free Clinic in San
Pedro, and owner of the Art Lab Gallery in San Pedro. Of note
was his active and honored participation in the American Cancer
Society and the Los Hermanos Fund. Originally from New York,
but a thirty-year resident of Rancho Palos Verdes, Block died
unexpectedly on January 29, 2005, at age seventy-two.

Nobody uses cultural symbols to achieve patient compliance
like **Dr. America Bracho** ("Tamales for Health"). Her work as
executive director of Latino Health Access, in Orange County,
involves her in one of the most frustrating areas for a health practitioner: achieving patient compliance in the control of chronic
disease. Bracho's award-winning diabetes management program
at Latino Health Access has had remarkable success. Physicians
who treat graduates of Bracho's program tell her they delight in
working with "active, informed, capable patients." But achieving
this level of patient involvement demands an equal commitment
from the practitioner, and Bracho gives it. She is not afraid to sing

with patients in her weekly two-hour educational sessions, or to teach them how to read numbers so they can read their glucose meter, or to spend a Sunday cooking and selling *tamales* to raise money for more outreach efforts. Bracho, a physician born in Venezuela, had never had a *tamal* until she immigrated to this country, but because Mexican culture predominates in Southern California, she threw herself into it. She stresses, in her narrative, the power that comes from understanding—of culture, of illness, of self. "I am convinced that people can learn and transform their lives," she says. "Education, when done appropriately, is a liberating process. Through our classes, I have witnessed how patients blossom and learn to control their disease. I have seen them making decisions and taking action to improve their lives. I want to share this experience." Bracho, MD, CEO of Latino Health Access in Santa Ana, California, received her medical degree from the Universidad Central de Venezuela before coming to the United States. Once here, her focus shifted to public health, and she obtained an MPH from the School of Public Health at the University of Michigan. Bracho directed programs in AIDS awareness and prevention in Detroit.

Medicine never requires a bigger human commitment than when the practitioner must confront a dying patient. Understanding the attendant fear and sadness requires a special sensitivity; statistical or therapeutic knowledge alone will not suffice. What dying patients want is a physician who will help them enrich their lives in those final moments. **Dr. Mercedes Brenneisen-Goode** ("We Talked about Our Lives, Our Dreams, Our Disappointments") has that capacity. For this, she has been honored by the American Cancer Society with its Hermanos En La Lucha Contra El Cancer (United in the Fight against Cancer) award. Brenneisen-Goode explains that while Latino patients, like any others, literally put their lives in the hands of their doctors, their lack of sophistication in understanding high technology medical methods makes them more vulnerable than others to confusion and despair. She uses a special sensitivity to navigate this delicate territory, which she sums up this way: "Compassionate listening is a gift which becomes more valuable the more I use it." Brenneisen-Goode, born and educated in Peru, comments that the continual presence of pain is an especially challenging aspect of oncology, for both patient and physician. Her solution has been to become vitally involved with her patients, to the extent of sharing her own religious beliefs with them. Any treatment methodologies patients find effective, whether they involve medical or spiritual care, receive her endorsement. Brenneisen-Goode feels that Latino cancer patients often find the *curandero* more successful than the traditional physician at controlling their pain, because the rituals and ceremonies essential to the *curandero's* craft give the patient a sense of participation and control. It is her wish that all caregivers recognize the importance of showing "kindness, sensitivity, and a humble attitude" in treating their patients. "Our modus operandi," she states, "should be to palliate both physical and spiritual pain." Brenneisen-Goode, MD, FACP, received her medical degree at the University of Southern California, where she was an associate professor of medicine. Dr. Brenneisen-Goode was in private practice in Los Angeles and Glendale, California, for twenty-five years, specializing in medical oncology and serving a mostly Latino client base. She retired in 2006 and started a new phase of her life—educating individuals in preventive medicine and natural healing through nutrition. Her hope is to change lives through patient participation in the outcome of their illnesses.

Affection should not remove the distance or respect that has to exist within the patient-physician relationship. **Dr. Graciela Calatayud** ("La Quinceañera") has the ability to be affectionate toward her patients while still being loved and respected. In her narrative about a young patient named Concepción, she shows how she is able to talk to an adolescent, slowly building trust, and eventually achieving compliance. Teenagers in Latino families frequently are confronted by a conflict in values: their parents' values, rooted in conservative, rural, Catholic Mexico, and modern American teen values, rooted in rap music, MTV, and commercial acquisition. For these teenagers, "Cielito Lindo" and Madonna are very close to each other—yet how many American teenagers share even popular music with their parents? The simple, yet not widely acknowledged fact of the Latino teenager's dual culture could be the source of both medical noncompliance and risk behavior in this group. Calatayud, a Mexican physician raised in Baja California who immigrated to the United States, has mastered cultural competence regarding the Latino teenager in the United States. She can success-fully create the environment of understanding and knowledge that is necessary to establish good lines of communication with these youngsters. She considers her role as a pediatrician to include a great deal of counseling and guidance for parents, helping them understand the importance of clear communication with their chil-dren as they enter the trying years of adolescence. And when the parents don't understand the culture that engulfs their children, they need more than ever the services of an experienced guide and mentor like Calatayud. Calatayud attended the Universidad Autonoma de Baja California in Mexicali, Mexico, before receiving her MD from Drew University School of Medical Science/Martin Luther King Jr. Hospital in Madison, New Jersey. She is currently in private practice in Huntington Park, California, where she has served as a pediatrician and general practitioner to the area's major-ity Latino population for the last fourteen years.

Anyone working in medicine has faced the difficult task of informing the family that their loved one will die, or has died. Even more difficult is approaching a family member in order to request the donation of an organ. In "Silence," **Rev. Luz Dillary Diaz** explains why this request may be even more difficult for Latinos. In many Latino cultures, the human body is considered to have two integral parts: the organs and the soul. After death, Latinos believe that the soul may remain in some of the organs, particularly the heart (considered the center of the soul) or the liver (where spilled bile can result in an "angry personality" or conditions triggered by such anger). Therefore, the donation of an organ from one individual to another has ramifications that go beyond the physical act. In a detailed interview, Diaz tells how she approaches the family of a potential donor. She is empathetic, and she is constantly aware of how delicate the approach must be. She touches the spiritual element necessary to win their confidence and again emphasizes the importance of faith and religion in winning the trust of Latino families. After gaining their confidence, she can broach the topic of an organ donation, largely stressing the happiness of the future recipient. Diaz is an ordained nondenominational minister who serves as an aftercare specialist for OneLegacy, a transplant donor network in Southern California. Diaz received her MA and Educational Specialist degrees from Loma Linda University in Southern California and trained as a hospital chaplain at Loma Linda and UCLA Medical Centers. She is currently studying for her MA in bioethics at Loyola Marymount University in Los Angeles, California.

Nothing is more intimidating and frightening than a hospital. The majority of immigrant Latinos traditionally experience their medical care in a small clinic or *consultorio*, with an empathic local physician. In recent years, an impersonal system of large clinics has developed in urban areas south of the border that some groups have tried to emulate in Los Angeles. The majority of indigent patients, therefore, must visit large, bureaucratic, cold, county hospitals. Once they reach them, they may lose their bearings. **Ted Estrada** ("Qué Grande Es el Hospital"), a Texas Mexican American, has worked to humanize hospital care in Latino areas. Estrada was initiated into the mysteries of the medical profession when, as a boy, he accompanied his great-grandmother on her midwife's rounds. This experience—including carrying home the "hams, vegetables or live chickens" with which she was sometimes paid—established an early interest in health care. An avid reader of everything Mexican, from Carlos Fuentes and Octavio Paz to Laura Esquivel (author of *Like Water for Chocolate*), Estrada has brought heightened cultural sensitivity to every hospital where he has been the administrator. In fact, the infamous hospital menu has been one area of attention for Estrada. Why would a patient faced with the trauma of a hospital stay eat foods she had never tasted before—in one of Estrada's stories, broccoli and mashed potatoes? Couldn't she have some *caldo de pollo* with fresh cilantro? Estrada claims that increased cultural competence in hospital administrators and personnel can be achieved "with no more than an investment of time and empathy." Still, Estrada has learned a few lessons the hard way. The reader will enjoy his adventures with an amputated arm. Estrada, senior vice president of hospital operations with International Hospital Corporation and CEO of IHC's Hospital Cima Hermosillo in Sonora, Mexico, was the CEO of East Los Angeles Doctors Hospital for seventeen years. He received his BA from the University of Texas, where he specialized in anthropology and the sciences, and has studied hospital administration at UCLA. Estrada has held positions at several hospitals in largely Latino areas in California, where he has been an active proponent of language and cultural sensitivity training for hospital staff members. He has been active in mentoring young Latinos who want to enter health care administration and is currently writing a book about his experiences as a hospital administrator in the Latino community.

Offenses that occur between a physician and a patient frequently are the result of poor communication. But this may be a matter not so much of language as it is of cultural-psychological knowledge. In spite of what is commonly taught about modern medical diagnostic and therapeutic methods, ultimately what patients want is a doctor who is available, who treats them with compassion, and who tries to open a path through the thicket of modern medical care. That is precisely what **Dr. Camilo Jorge** ("No Ofendas") has done for his patients for over fifty years of medical practice. Jorge, a native of the Dominican Republic who primarily practices medicine with Mexican-origin Latino patients in Los Angeles County, has many of the qualities of a great physician. One quality that stands out in his narrative is his understanding of the mentality of Latino patients. This is no more than the difficult task of perceiving what the patient truly wants from a doctor. The title of his narrative tells how Jorge obtains compliance without difficulty: he never offends. What this means in practice is that Jorge listens carefully and respectfully, treats even the humblest of his patients without arrogance, and acknowledges the patient's fears and apprehensions, no matter how rooted in superstition. Thus, like other Latino physicians, he frequently shares with a healer or *curandero* in the treatment of folk ailments. Revered by his patients, Jorge may be the last link to the traditional Latin American humanist healer, as much poet as priest, as much surgeon as storyteller. Jorge attended the University of Santo Domingo in the Dominican Republic, where he received his MD. He is a physician and surgeon with a private practice in Los Angeles County, California, where perhaps 75 percent of his clients are Latino.

The coeditor of this volume, **Dr. David E. Hayes-Bautista**, PhD, is professor of medicine in the UCLA Division of General Internal Medicine and director of the Center for the Study of Latino Health and Culture in the David Geffen School of Medicine at UCLA. He is on the boards of the California Latino Medical Association. He received his BA in sociology from the University of California, Berkeley, and his MA and PhD in medical sociology from the University of California, San Francisco. He is the author of *La Nueva California: Latinos in the Golden State*, published by University of California Press.

Dr. Margarita Keusayan ("La Mujer") agrees with Dr. Jorge that all caregivers should include prudence and respect in their daily practice. Physicians with an abrupt manner, who spend only a short time with each patient, frequently find themselves faced with the "unhappy patient." Keusayan went so far as to say "I become part of my patient; I feel the patient's anguish and share in his suffering." With this philosophy, she practiced family medicine in a heavily Latino population in Los Angeles, California. Her successful practice was achieved after years of struggle. In 1958 she entered the University of the Republic of Uruguay and emerged ten years later with a medical degree "that many said was unobtainable by a woman." In 1972, with two children and a third on the way, Keusayan and her husband embarked upon a new challenge: they left for the United States where, after another four years of study, she obtained her American MD. Keusayan commented that her thirty years as a physician enabled her to grow personally and to give back to the Latino community. Her narrative tells of the variety of situations that a general practitioner in a small clinic serving the underprivileged finds herself in, and how she applied psychological, spiritual, and medical means to relieve her patients' woes. Keusayan came from Montevideo, Uruguay. After receiving her MD and spending several years in emergency room and private practice in Uruguay, Dr. Keusayan and her family returned to the United States, where she again became a licensed physician. She was director of Clínica Santa Clara, a private medical clinic in a low-income, primarily Latino area of Los Angeles. She passed away in 2000.

The spiritual importance of the heart to the Latino is a daily challenge for **Dr. Ismael Navarro Nuño** ("Que Dios Guíe Sus Manos"). Nuño is the chief of cardiac surgery in one of the busiest and most intense hospitals in the country, the vast, gigantic Los Angeles County/USC Medical Center. Yet an illustrious career has not distracted him from his cultural origins. As he stares out from his tenth-floor window at the lights of an enormous city sprawling below him, he contemplates how far the young boy from Tijuana, Mexico, who threw rocks at patrolling *migra* cars and carried a toy doctor's bag, has come. After medical school in Guadalajara and specialized training in general surgery at UC San Diego and in cardiac surgery at the Walter Reed Army Medical Center in Washington, D.C., Nuño then served at a variety of military posts both here and abroad. His active career as a military doctor included service at the Presidio in San Francisco, California, at Heidelberg, Germany, and as medical commander of the Fifth MASH during the Gulf War of 1990–91. When Nuño discusses with his patients the tremendous risks that cardiovascular surgery carries with it, he does it with a full awareness of the centrality of the heart for the Latino patient. He expects patients to wonder whether their beloved father, mother, brother, or sister will change as a result of his work. But he acknowledges, and responds to, these concerns with a warmth born of understanding and identification. In his narrative, Nuño describes dramatic experiences of life and death. But, throughout, it is evident that he understands the hierarchy of the family, the cultural needs and spiritual desires of his patients. For both doctor and patient, he feels, religious faith is paramount in the success of his difficult operations. As a symbol of unity of skill and spirituality in his practice, Nuño begins any surgery by making the sign of the cross over the patient's heart with his sterile, gloved hand. Nuño, MD, FACS, FACC, FACCP, is immediate past president of the American Heart Association for the Western States Affiliate.

While working with battered women through the L.A. Commission on Assaults against Women, **Cristina Orcí Fernández** ("Discovering Curanderismo") discovered that there is much more to healing than physical recovery. Her involvement in health led her to become a self-defense instructor, a Hellerwork Structural Integration practitioner, and an expert on *curanderismo*. Despite growing up as a first-generation Mexican American with a grand-mother who brewed herbal remedies, Orcí Fernández says that *curanderismo* was a mystery to her until she began studying it while living from 1992 to 1997 in Chiapas, a Mexican state renowned for its richness, beauty, and political unrest. Here, she found a wide variety of healers and began consulting them, as well as the local physicians, in an attempt to improve health care in the area. "It was a joyful discovery," Orcí Fernández writes. "This incredible network (of my own making!) of healers who have such different approaches but in the end, take care of the whole person." In her chapter, Orcí Fernández details the kinds of healers involved in *curanderismo* and tells of the development of the Health Promoters System, which brings medical services to rural areas all over the world. Orcí Fernández's work with K'inal Antzetik, a nonprofit group dedicated to improving the health of Indian women in the Chiapas highlands, showed her how traditional medicine and Western medicine can coexist and enrich each other—both in Mexico and in Latino communities here in the United States. Orcí Fernández spent most of her youth in Mexico City. She has a BA in French literature from Pomona College. She is now a copywriter with La Agencia de Orcí, a Los Angeles-based advertising agency.

Fantasy and magic are, perhaps, as integral to Latino culture as religion is. A sense of fantasy is as important as the taste of food, or the appearance of a building, or the sound of music. Caribbean Latinos share a wildly complex cultural melting pot, including African, Dutch, and French influences as well as the Spanish and Indian influences that predominate elsewhere, and magic is the common denominator. **Dr. Angel Ponce** ("Magic and Medicine"), a second-generation physician from the Dominican Republic, explains his own origins and also untangles this seem-ingly confusing cultural mélange. He understands that in spite of attempts to generalize Latino patients, there are as many differences as similarities. However, all share a strong cultural commitment to mystic values. Ponce, MD, a medical oncologist, is currently chief of staff at Suburban Medical Center in Paramount, California, and is on staff at Harbor–UCLA Medical Center, St. Francis Medical Center, and Martin Luther King/Drew Medical Center, all in Southern California. Dr. Ponce attended the Universidad Autonoma de Santo Domingo, in the Dominican Republic, and trained in internal medicine at the University of Maryland Hospital in Baltimore and medical oncology at Harbor–UCLA Medical Center.

Second-generation Mexican American **Irene Redondo-Churchward** (*Cada Cabeza Es Un Mundo*), a native of Tucson, Arizona, maintains a close connection with her ancestral heritage. Despite these strong emotional ties, Redondo-Churchward lives the dichotomy between traditional Latino culture and our pluralistic society. Latinos who grow up, as she did, in a sometimes inimical American culture, often absorb traditional attitudes and attributes through *dichos* (sayings) passed from family to family, from generation to generation. These simple words, Redondo-Churchward tells us, reflect the daily behavior of Latinos and sculpt the lives of individuals. She is now executive director of SPIRITT Family Services in Whittier, Los Angeles County, a community services center that provides a range of family preservation services—alcohol and drug intervention and treatment, child abuse prevention, domestic violence counseling, youth empowerment, and job training—to a largely Latino population. Her narrative analyzes in depth which factors lead to addictive behavior in the *borracho*, or Latino alcoholic. She describes the extremes, from the *pesado* (overbearing drunk) to the abusive wife-beater that, unfortunately, we all too frequently observe in every community. Redondo-Churchward explains that the glorification of alcohol in Mexican music, movies, and media reinforces the cultural acceptability of alcohol use in periods of frustration and sadness, happiness and triumph. Drinking, she reports, plays a significant role in the *macho* personality that so many Latino men cultivate. Such an individual is physically aggressive, domineering, arrogant, and frequently a womanizer, and prides himself on the consumption of liquor. Thus, many Latinos closely associate alcohol consumption with manhood. Alcohol use in Latinas, however, reflects a form of acculturation, since it is not similarly accepted in Latino culture. Latinas frequently hide their drinking and drink alone. They may ignore or deny the problem and frequently feel ashamed of having violated the sacredness of the mother-image that is dear to many Latinos. Redondo-Churchward has been active in the field of human services for over twenty years and has done pioneering work in establishing programs to treat alcoholism in Latinas. She was selected as one of six women to represent the United States at the Japan/U.S. Women Leaders' Dialogue, was one of the twenty-five women participating in the National Hispana Leadership Institute coordinated with Harvard's JFK School of Government, and has been honored by *Hispanic* magazine for her work with families and children. Redondo-Churchward has received numerous awards for leadership, most recently the Las Distinguidas 1997 award from the American Association of University Women.

Dr. Felipe O. Santana ("Dolor de Cabeza") begins our book with a story of self-discovery. Born to an impoverished family in Cuba, Santana ultimately earned a doctorate in psychology from the University of Havana before arriving as a political refugee in the United States. In his subsequent private practice in Los Angeles, Santana treated a mainly Anglo population. But upon his retirement, Dr. Santana became a psychotherapist at Clinicas del Camino Real, a nonprofit organization in Ventura County, California, offering comprehensive services to the poor, mostly Latino, and largely migrant population of this agricultural area. Here, Santana quickly discovered that the skills he had developed over a career with a better-educated population availed him little. By returning to his roots—by remembering his mother's words—Santana discovers a method that is both "profound and simple" to understand and resolve the problems that his patients face. What is this method? Santana listens and observes, and conducts a gentle, respectful conversation. He lets his patients tell their stories in their own way—and in their own time. "The well-to-do and school-educated consider this method a waste of time, and time is money," Santana writes. "But with the Latino culture on which we are focusing, this personal approach has a great value." His personal tone rapidly achieves the rapport necessary to have access to the most intimate part of his patients' lives. Santana describes particular aspects of Latino culture that are likely to appear in the consulting room. He acknowledges the use of *chistes* (jokes) by Latinos even in the most difficult periods of their lives. He stresses that the religious and social hierarchy of Latino culture also affects patient-caregiver interactions and cautions practitioners to understand that the priest and the doctor are closely allied in the mind of the patient. His narrative reaffirms the importance of family as an integral part of the Latino problem-solving equation. Santana, PHD, MFCT, a former faculty member of the UCLA Department of Psychiatry, School of Medicine, was also an administrator in the Department of Alcohol and Drug Programs of Ventura County.

Rev. Norbert Sharon, ST ("A Gallon of Healing"), pastor of Our Lady of Victory Church in Compton (an inner-city parish in Southern California) has spent most of his adult life offering religious support to Latinos as a missionary priest for the poor. Born in Chicago, he studied at Catholic University, Washington, D.C.; at Javariana University in Bogotá, Colombia; and at the Mexican-American Cultural Institute in San Antonio, Texas. He has traveled extensively in Latin American countries, in communities where poverty prevailed, and in his career has mainly been assigned to

Latino parishes. He has learned from his parishioners how to approach Latinos in their moments of sadness, stress, and death. Despite his thick Spanish accent (which, he claims, everyone is afraid to correct), he transmits a special warmth and has changed the lives of many. In his narrative, he describes how a young boy with a terminal illness embraced faith and religion to endure his suffering, confirming that faith and religion are essential ingredients for Latino healing. In a humbling anecdote, Father Norbert recounts how he learned the value of a gallon of holy water.

Hungarian by birth but Mexican by education and inclination, **Kati Szamos** ("Tacos Dorados No More") became fascinated by the complex textures and exquisite flavors of the cuisine of her adopted country, Mexico. Szamos became a nutritionist with a special interest in the dietary deficiencies that exist in Latin American countries. She has devoted her life to improving Latino health where it starts—in the kitchen. As a nutrition consultant and educator, Szamos believes in balance and knows that eating right has more to do with culture and habits than with economics. She notes that the three basic components of Mexican cuisine—corn, beans, and chili—are nearly always served in a Latino home, even in the United States. In her story, Szamos tells how she manages to improve the diet and health consciousness of a Mexican immigrant and his family residing in Los Angeles. People don't change lifelong eating habits overnight—and Szamos quickly realizes that if she fulfills her client's expectations and puts him on a diet that denies him his favorite foods, she will accomplish nothing. Instead, Szamos works with the entire family, uncovering the sources of their eating patterns and showing them new ways to enjoy the foods they love. Szamos lets the family choose recipes that appeal to them, then teaches healthful yet flavorful ways to cook. Spending time with the family, cooking and eating with them, Szamos gently wins them over to healthy ways of eating. In addition to her teaching and

consulting, Szamos has written four books in Spanish on nutrition and is the author of over 200 articles on the subject. She is
also a frequent guest on radio and television programs in both
Los Angeles and Mexico, has appeared three times on *Sábado
Gigante*, and has hosted a nutrition advice program for Televisa
in Mexico City. Born in Budapest, Szamos studied nutrition and
psychology in Mexico. She was a case manager in the Diabetes
Prevention Research Program at UCLA but now works in the
Keck School of Medicine at USC. She is nutrition research
manager for an eleven-year research study that follows 5,000
participants nationwide to track the outcome of weight loss and
physical activity on individuals who are overweight, over the age
of fifty-five and have diabetes. She heads the group of dietitians,
physical fitness experts and psychologists who work with the
study participants. Since 2003, Szamos (now Konersman) has
had a weekly column in *La Opinión* (Southern California's best-
known Spanish-language newspaper) and continues to publish
her columns on health and nutrition in several editorial pages
throughout Latin America.

  Dr. Arturo Velazquez Jr. ("Mexican or Mexican American?") has
found that understanding whether he is dealing with a "Mexican,"
a "Chicano," or a "Mexican American" helps him provide appropriate, culturally sensitive care to Latino clients (mostly of Mexican
origin) in his private practice in West Covina, a suburb of Los
Angeles. These three groups, distinguished by different levels of
familiarity with and understanding of American society, all share
the values that characterize Latinos: a deep sense of religion, close
family bonds, respect and loyalty to friends. Velazquez's story clari-
fies how health care is perceived by the groups he identifies. The
new immigrant is respectful, sometimes submissive, often afraid
of new technologies, and frequently resorts to alternative care. At
the other extreme, Velazquez notes, the Chicano is knowledgeable,
demanding, not easily satisfied. Velazquez, a family practitioner

born in Los Angeles but raised in Mexico and educated in both places, has achieved the cultural competence that allows him to understand the psychology of both Latino and American cultures. He describes the approaches he takes with each group. Even his initial decision of whether to address a patient in Spanish or English may have treatment ramifications. Spanish, respected as the language of their elders, is effective as a way of achieving compliance in his Mexican American patients; however, second- or third-generation Latinos, who identify themselves as American, may be insulted by his addressing them in Spanish, considering it an implication that their English is faulty. Likewise, his approach to alternative kinds of healing (*sobadoras*, *curanderas*, *yerberas*, and other curers and herbalists) varies, depending on the patient's physical and psychological needs, and he has been known to surprise patients by prescribing oregano tea to relieve coughs. Velazquez, MD, chose to attend medical school at the Universidad Autonoma de Baja California, feeling that the best preparation for a career in the Latino community would be in a Mexican setting. Dr. Velazquez did his social service internship in Baja California before his American residency at hospitals in Michigan and Wisconsin. Currently, he has a solo family practice in West Covina, California, where his patients are almost all Latino.

Finally, **Dr. Juan Villagomez** ("Si Dios Nos Da Licensia"), a general practitioner specializing in geriatrics, touches upon Saint Luke's injunction, "Physician, heal thyself." This well-respected Los Angeles-area physician, a man who worked the vineyards of Napa and Mendocino Counties as a boy, who twice bicycled in the grueling 525-mile California AIDS Ride, was diagnosed with adenocarcinoma in June 1996. Villagomez felt the pain and nausea brought on by chemotherapy and other invasive procedures. He experienced the depression, even despair, of a cancer diagnosis. Yet, as Villagomez writes, "On the Monday morning after my diagnosis, I tried to resume being a doctor." Ironically, while Villagomez was fighting his own illness, he treated an elderly woman with a similar condition, stomach cancer. Despite the anguish of watching her die while he responded well to his own treatment, Villagomez gained strength and perspective from the experience. He tells us that Mrs. Marmolejo continued to treat him with humor and kindness, sharing her stock of "X-rated" jokes that Villagomez wishes he had recorded. The doctor shared the patient's world: like her, he received comfort from friends and family, felt the solace of religion, and sometimes cried in despair. After his diagnosis, when Villagomez had returned to practice, he found it harder to maintain the physician's balance between empathy and objectivity in treating the patients he then diagnosed with cancer. But he approached each of his patients "with compassion and hope," providing us with the ultimate example of the empathy that cultural understanding awakens in the compassionate practitioner. Before he passed away in 1999, he was honored with the Humanitarian Award by the National Council of Christians and Jews and the first-ever "Por Ecclesia y Pontifice" Award for laymen in the Catholic Church. He also served as the first president of the new California Latino Medical Association (CaLMA), which he had worked tirelessly to bring about. Villagomez, MD, shared a family practice with three other physicians in West Los Angeles. Some 80 percent of his patients were Latino and about half were elderly. After graduating from Santa Clara University, Dr. Villagomez received his MD from University of California at San Francisco School of Medicine and did his family practice residency at Santa Monica Hospital. He had teaching affiliations with the family practice departments at both University of Southern California and UCLA Medical Schools.

* * *

The loss of our good friend and the coeditor of this volume has been felt by many. **Dr. Roberto Chiprut** ("Body and Soul") was an internist and gastroenterologist attending at Cedars-Sinai Medical Center in Los Angeles and associate clinical professor in the UCLA Department of Medicine. He received his MD from the Universidad Nacional Autonoma de Mexico, and completed training in medicine and gastroenterology at the Scott and White Clinic at Baylor University, and in hepatology at Jackson Memorial Hospital at the University of Miami. Chiprut was a fellow of the American College of Physicians and the American College of Gastroenterology. He was also past president and chairman of Brothers in the Fight against Cancer of the American Cancer Society, and president and chairman of Latino Care IPA. Please see the "In Memoriam" section.

David E. Hayes-Bautista

Introduction
Lessons in Latino Cultural Competency

David E. Hayes-Bautista

> Culture is a society's style, its way of living and dying. It embraces the erotic and the culinary arts; dancing and burial; courtesy and curses; work and leisure; rituals and festivals; punishments and rewards; dealings with the dead and with the ghosts who people our dreams; attitudes toward women and children, old people and strangers, enemies and allies; eternity and the present; the here and now and the beyond.
>
> Octavio Paz, *The Labyrinth of Solitude*

*U*sually, we only become aware of culture through the absence of our own. When we travel to another country, we experience "culture shock": people eat strange foods, stand closer together or farther apart, drive on the wrong side of the street, rattle along in unknown tongues, or laugh at political cartoons in the newspapers that we can't understand. Adventurous travelers find this culture clash stimulating; still, most will wonder why these people can't do things "just like back home." Our own way of doing things seems logical, rational, full of common sense.

Immigrants experience the same shock, although unlike tourists who return home in a matter of days or weeks, their malaise may be long lasting. Immigrant groups have traditionally mitigated the shock of immersion in a foreign culture by gathering in comforting enclaves of familiar languages, foods, dress, and manners. Ultimately, when the immigrant group becomes large enough, its culture spills out into the larger community and effects changes in it. In twenty-first-century America, such cultural intermingling is occurring at an ever-faster pace.

The Latino population in the United States, as of 2004, is the nation's largest, and most rapidly growing, minority. Over 40 million strong at the time of this printing, it is estimated that there will be around 110 million Latinos in the United States by 2050. Beginning with the third quarter of 2001, over 50 percent of the babies born in California were Latino. In essence, one out of every four Americans will be of Latino ancestry by the middle of this century (Hayes-Bautista 2004). As American society becomes increasingly diverse, the non-Latino population has begun to understand that Latinos share a culture that involves not just preferences in food and music, but "commonsense" notions of how to perform life's daily activities. As the Latino population rises, market-driven institutions quickly respond: radio stations shift their play lists from English to Spanish; supermarkets increase the quality and selection of tortillas; department stores boost their stock of frilly baptismal, first communion, and *quinceañera* dresses; restaurants cater to tastes for specific types of Latino cuisine such as that of Oaxaca, the Yucatán, and the Andes. Organizations that serve the public—in fields as diverse as education, government, and the media—find it ethically appropriate and financially prudent to tailor their services to the changing marketplace. Many industries have launched marketing initiatives based on painstaking research on Latino consumer choices in home furnishings, foods, apparel, automobiles, music, even home mortgages.

Unfortunately, such research has not typically been done in the health care industry. Most health care providers and researchers are aware that Latino patients bring unique views of health and illness to the examination room. However, beyond texts of medical Spanish and some anthropological work, there is little literature on what a provider should do to increase comfort, effective treatment, and patient compliance with Latinos. This book, *Healing Latinos: Realidad y Fantasía*, was written by physicians and providers to fill that need. We, the editors, secured the participation of seventeen colleagues who wanted to share their stories. Most are currently in practice in Southern California and come from a variety of training backgrounds, some U.S.-based, others in Mexico or in Latin America. Our goal is to help our colleagues practice culturally effective medicine with their Latino patients. Something more than broad market responses are needed to create successful personal interactions. Health care providers and medical care organizations, from solo providers to multisite HMOs, must learn to adjust to group dynamics and individual preferences. They will need to understand Latino culture more intimately than, for example, a grocery store that can attract customers simply by increasing the variety of its goods.

Cultural Patterns of Behavior

During a typical day, we all make thousands of behavioral decisions without giving them much thought. We choose what to wear, what to eat, which route to drive to work, when to tell a joke. Each decision is small, yet aggregated over the course of a day, each reflects our individual internalization of cultural patterns.

Every culture carries its own patterns, which its members use to understand and respond to the world. Psychological research on memory and knowledge has demonstrated that when material is organized into recognizable designs, it is more easily retained. Our cultural patterns help us organize and store knowledge in quickly retrievable forms. Thus, culture provides a shorthand mode of dealing with the overwhelming mass of detail that makes up the real world. Cultural patterns help individuals quickly organize and sort the events in the world, so that they act in a way that is seemingly instinctive, yet in harmony with the expectations of others. Informally derived and unconsciously learned cultural patterns guide most of the daily activities of life. Humans learn these cultural patterns from the moment of birth. Parents, siblings, relatives, friends, schoolmates, neighbors, teachers, and coworkers, as well as newspapers, television programs, and song lyrics, are all sources of cultural information that provide an individual with patterns of behavior, emotion, and knowledge.

Cultural Patterns of Emotion

Emotions are basic to all human beings. But emotions are very much conditioned by culture. As Octavio Paz points out, culture directs what we feel about life events and how we react to them. The specific images, perceptions, and events that trigger emotions vary from culture to culture and are communicated effectively through symbols. Each symbol, whether it is visual or aural, encapsulates a lengthy cultural memory and is meant to trigger a strong emotion. Baseball, hot dogs, and apple pie symbolize home and country for many Americans. For Latinos, the Virgin of Guadalupe is an equally powerful symbol, shorthand for comfort, home, and community.

Words are another powerful way to stir up emotions about home. *Wetback, illegal, invader:* these words triggered the powerful, negative emotions that led to the passage of Proposition

187, which restricted government-provided services to non-citizens in California in 1994.

Gestures also communicate emotions about home. The French and the Italians have an extensive, expressive range of gestures; American culture, although somewhat impoverished in this regard, can claim an emphatic example in the upraised middle finger. More subtle but equally communicative gestures that signal the inside of the home culture (in contrast to the outside of foreign cultures) are the timing and placement of the smile, the upraised eyebrow, the posture of the arms. An *abrazo* (embrace), a *grito* (cry) during a heartrending mariachi song, or the touch of a hand on an arm at the right moment—all communicate belonging for Latinos.

Cultural Patterns of Knowledge

Not only behavior and emotion are culturally marked—so is knowledge. Most cultural knowledge is informal: never written down, never studied by academics, yet ubiquitous. This knowledge, passed from parent to child, shared among friends, sets the boundaries for particular social interactions. A much smaller part of a culture's knowledge is written down and subjected to formal rules of discovery and proof.

In U.S. Anglo culture, medicine is a form of cultural knowledge that is written down. One must study for years and pass a number of tests to ensure mastery of this formal body of knowledge. In Latino lay culture, there is little formal health knowledge. Most awareness of health and illness is informal; for example:

• A *susto* (fright) can cause an onset of diabetes.
• A baby taken out bareheaded in cold weather will catch a cold.
• *Uña de gato* (a South American herb) is a sure remedy for many illnesses.

The History of Latino Cultural Patterns

To summarize, the three main building blocks of culture are patterns of behavior, emotion, and knowledge. None of them is created afresh with each new generation. Instead, these patterns have histories, some of them very lengthy, as in the case of Latinos.

Much of Latino culture in the United States grows out of cultural development in the Mesoamerican plateaus dating back 50,000 years. Latino culture results from centuries of accreting patterns of behavior, emotion, and knowledge from a variety of groups, including the Spanish, who brought a language and a religion; the Africans, who brought food, gods, and rhythms; and Anglo Americans, who beamed new tastes and attitudes into Latino homes from Miami to Buenos Aires.

When a pregnant Latina avoids going out during a full moon, gives up the pleasures of gum chewing, wears a red thread around her abdomen, and yet wants to see her sonogram and practice Lamaze techniques, she embodies the continuity and change that characterize Latino culture. When two Latino men greet each other with a hearty, two-armed hug (*abrazo*), they are behaving in accordance with their culture. When an Anglo turns his or her back on a Latino, the Latino experiences this as an insult, a cultural expression that denies his or her very existence.

The Cultural Patterns of the Medical Profession

In medicine, as in other disciplines from music to mathematics, students learn specific cultural patterns that allow them to see designs in the cacophony of information around them and allow them to make instantaneous decisions about what behaviors to take, what emotions to feel, and what knowledge to apply.

Medical practitioners use specialized patterns to select the medical knowledge most relevant to the situation at hand. When a patient complains of chest pain, for example, one protocol is appropriate if the physician suspects heartburn, another if the physician suspects a potentially serious heart condition. Practitioners balance basic patterns with concern for individual differences, as no two patients are completely alike. Yet, for all their idiosyncrasies, patients are enough alike that one can—and must—start with some general patterns.

When a provider and a patient are in the same examination room, two distinct cultural languages interact:

• The provider's understanding of the illness and the patient.

• The patient's understanding of the illness, the provider, and the patient's own world.

The provider's cultural understanding includes formal medical procedures that are disease-specific and formal guidelines for treating patients. But the provider's informal cultural guidelines—including the provider's notions about the patient—may be just as significant. When the provider and the patient don't share an informal cultural understanding, confusion, discomfort, and dissatisfaction may be the result. This is why *cultural competency*—an understanding of the relevant, informal cultural language of a large patient base—is so critical in today's diverse world.

Rarely does a patient change diet or stop smoking simply because "the doctor told me to." When prevention is the strategy—as it is for many chronic diseases—then providers need to develop a new specialty: the ability to elicit patient involvement. If the patient's attention can be engaged, if the patient's emotions become involved and skill levels increase, then there is a greater probability of seeing the deep-seated, permanent changes in behavior that will have an effect on disease patterns and, ultimately, on the services demanded.

Understanding Cultural Patterns versus Imposing Stereotypes

Some observers are concerned that encouraging physicians to understand the cultural patterns of one of their patient groups may simply be supporting a not-so-sophisticated form of stereotyping. Stereotypes do, in fact, involve an attempt to understand behavior that is foreign. But, because stereotypes come from outside the cultural group, attempting to explain unknown phenomena, stereotypes are oversimplified, inexact, and frequently pejorative. Lacking relevant cultural information, people resort to crude approximations that often stigmatize. In this sense, cultural competency can be attained only when stereotypes have been abolished. Foreigners should not evaluate the attitudes and behavior of an unfamiliar cultural group.

For instance, in a historic survey in Southern California, about half of the non-Hispanic whites surveyed felt that the stereotypes of Latinos engendered by that decade's public policy debate (Latinos are undocumented, or gang members, or welfare mothers) were accurate. However, the other half felt that these stereotypes did not accurately describe Latinos (Hurtado et al. 1992). Unfortunately, this group did not have an alternative image of Latinos that they could articulate. In effect, they had rejected a stereotype but did not yet understand the cultural patterns of the Latinos living among them, patterns that would enable Anglos to understand Latino thought and behavior.

For non-Latino medical providers, as for the general public, it is easy to fall back on stereotypes about Latino patients when they have limited or no knowledge of the relevant cultural patterns. Yet, medical providers have little difficulty individuating patients of their own cultural group. When providers and patients share cultural patterns, providers are able to treat each patient as an individual, an important goal in any medical practice.

What Latino Physicians Understand

The chapters in this book are written in a very personal way by a variety of medical providers—both Latino and non-Latino—who share their knowledge about how to approach Latino patients. Latino providers have an advantage over most non-Latino providers, in that they already share cultural patterns. In fact, recognizing the personal, Latino-Latino link is often the most important first step that the Latino provider can take with a new patient. For providers raised in either Mexico or Latin America, or in Latino families in the United States, the personal link is often obvious, even physical. Dr. Ismael Nuño, who works in cardiac surgery, writes in his chapter:

> Many of the little Mexican ladies remind me of my mother; the elderly men remind me of my father.
>
> Ismael Navarro Nuño

Often, because of the places where they train and practice, Latino providers may spend time away from Latino patients, family, and neighborhoods, and their link may become attenuated. However, once among Latino patients, the myriad subtle cues that are shared cultural inheritances remind the provider of this natural bond.

> I find that my knowledge of and firsthand experience with Mexican customs, national and religious holidays, and Mexico's political, educational, and health care systems help me in many cases to break the ice and form a common bond.
>
> Arturo Velazquez Jr.

Once the shared cultural patterns are recognized, shared designs begin to shape the interaction. While there are nearly infinite variations, cultural patterns provide meaning to the most mundane of behaviors: greeting a person, sharing food, recalling a memory. Once the Latino practitioner establishes this deep connection with a patient, a successful partnership begins to grow.

> For my Latino patients, it is precisely the ability to deal with these [emotional and cultural] issues that distinguishes a really effective physician.
>
> Mercedes Brenneisen-Goode

Fortunately, these advantages are available not only to those who are Latinos. While Latino providers already have an ingrained understanding of the relevant cultural patterns, any concerned provider can learn these patterns. All cultural patterns of behavior are learnable and, once learned, will help lessen the "foreignness" of Latino patients and allow individualized medical care to occur.

Acquiring Latino Cultural Competency

Medical organizations have sometimes attempted to promote cultural competency by providing lists of dos and don'ts regarding cultural behavior:

- Do look Latino patients in the eye.
- Don't look Asian patients in the eye.
- Do return nail clippings to Native American patients.

While a useful starting point, a long list of dos and don'ts can be daunting and confusing. Can Japanese and Chinese patients be looked in the eye? What about Vietnamese or Hmong? Should a second-generation Mexican American and a recently arrived immigrant from Nicaragua be treated the same way? Learning cultural patterns, rather than do's and don'ts, provides a more reliable basis for communication, as it keys providers to underlying patterns rather than specific situations.

But cultural patterns are not systematically taught in medical or health professional schools. Physicians generally begin their practice with few formal notions of cultural competency.

Latino physicians, like others, gradually learn that they must supplement their extensive formal knowledge with the informal cultural savvy that has, sometimes, been suppressed by the rigors of American-style medical training. They learn to reach back to their roots, to rely on their life experiences; gradually, the provider-patient relationship becomes a human-human one.

> Success . . . requires reaching into the hearts of the people and understanding their culture.
>
> Margarita Keusayan

Main Latino Cultural Patterns

The following chapters were written by Southern California providers about their experiences delivering care to Latino patients. The collection reflects the different backgrounds of the authors: each has a unique tale to tell. However, there are some approaches and patterns in the narratives that, taken together, can help us understand the unique qualities of Latino patients. This presentation of the main cultural patterns illustrated in the practitioners' narratives was achieved through a specific qualitative method called grounded theory (Glaser and Strauss 1967), which is designed to extract a level of abstraction from empirical experiences.

COMMUNICATION

Communication with Latino patients is something Latino providers pride themselves on. They recognize that many issues are complex, chronic, and emotionally charged, and that good communication is the only way to approach these subjects effectively. Communication, of course, is an important skill for physicians to practice with all patients, and it involves much more than language. Nevertheless, a special focus on communication is important for culturally competent physicians.

Language Choice

Latino patients may speak Spanish, English, or both. The first task in communication is to assess which language is best for the particular patient encounter. The very first spoken words may set the tone for the entire encounter. As one doctor puts it in his chapter of this book:

> If the [Latino] patient is English-speaking only, it can be the equivalent of a slap in the face if I don't speak English right off.
>
> Arturo Velazquez Jr.

Waiting room observations may help dictate the choice.

> When I hear them speaking in the waiting or examination rooms, I have some idea of what language to speak with them, even before the first introductions.
>
> Arturo Velazquez Jr.

The encounter may also be started with a simple, conscious probing.

> At our first meeting, I may start with a simple *buenos dias* or hello and then ask the nature of the visit.
>
> Arturo Velazquez Jr.

The response will often indicate the language of preference.

> Usually, the Spanish-dominant patient will politely ask me to speak Spanish. Those who are bilingual usually do not mind which language I use. Others will state the language they prefer.
>
> Arturo Velazquez Jr.

If providers are not fluent in Spanish, they cannot reasonably be expected to achieve fluency in a short period of time. Thus, some providers have to rely on interpreters. Having a third-party interpreter is better than having no communication, but it can create discomfort for the patient.

> For the most part, Mexicans would like to speak to their physician without a third party translating and thus becoming aware of some potentially embarrassing information.
>
> Arturo Velazquez Jr.

Active Listening

Once the language of the interview has been established, active listening will give the provider a second avenue of effective communication. For any provider with any patient, active listening is a recommended, and learnable, skill. Two phenomena are brought into play in successful listening. The first is language skill. If providers are fluent in both Spanish and English, language will not impede listening.

However, knowledge of the cultural patterns that organize a patient's life experiences is as important as language facility in effective listening. A patient's seemingly simple sentence can be the tip of a conceptual and emotional iceberg, made meaningful only by a familiarity with Latino cultural patterns.

> "Que Dios guíe sus manos" (May God guide your hands).
>
> Latino patient to Ismael Navarro Nuño

Far from an expression of fatalism, the young Latino surgeon to whom this phrase was uttered understood it as a statement of confidence: the only other person to whom the patient would trust his life is God.

Probing

Part of active listening is the ability to probe for information. Latino immigrant patients, in particular, may have rather indirect forms of speech. A familiarity with cultural patterns may provide clues that a provider should probe further.

> I had one patient come to see me in a very depressed state. At first I thought his condition was only depression. But as I sat and talked with him, the medical issue emerged: there was something wrong with his penis. Many Latinos, particularly Mexicans, would rather die than lose their potency. He considered his life practically over.
>
> Camilo Jorge

The providers writing in this book have learned that they often need to initiate the probing in a very indirect way.

> Assessment of the case is done indirectly…in a conversational fashion. The patient might say, "The doctor referred me to you. I have very strong headaches in the back of my head and sometimes I have stomach problems." My question is, "Then the doctor knows what is going on?" "Well, they think that it is my nerves." Not that they are depressed or anxious, but it is the patient's "nerves." Now the assessment begins to focus on the pathology.
>
> Felipe O. Santana

Even if they do not elicit useful information, carefully chosen questions show that the provider is interested and empathetic. Medicine touches on many areas of profound human emotion: the joy of birth, the fear of chronic disease, the pain of trauma, the finality of death. Good communication allows a provider to assist a patient through these emotions, make sense of them, and incorporate them, when appropriate, into the treatment regimen.

> I like to say that I become part of the patient; I feel the patient's anguish and share in his suffering.
>
> Margarita Keusayan

EMOTIONS

While Latinos are sometimes described as being more emotional than Anglos, it is probably more accurate to describe Latinos as having different cultural patterns of response in emotional situations. Emotions are an integral part of Latino health-seeking behavior. Emotions are also important in a clinical sense: the lives of many Latinos, especially immigrants, are stressful, and these stresses may become part of the medical problem.

> In a Latino patient base, there will be many patients who come in with largely psychosomatic, rather than medical, problems.
>
> Camilo Jorge

> When poor Latinos come to me for therapy, I know I am not dealing with headaches that are related to any type of chemical imbalance or organicity.
>
> Felipe O. Santana

> I have to determine early on if the patient comes in with a physical ailment, or a more psychological one.
>
> Camilo Jorge

Emotionally related conditions may be of two types. The first is emotion as a problem in and of itself. A common nonspecific complaint of Latinos is *nervios*—literally, nerves.

> A great number of the patients who come to my office exhibit psychosomatic symptoms, usually what they call *nervios*, often the result of the worries and stresses of their lives.
>
> Camilo Jorge

Latino providers are quick to point out that these conditions are real for the patient and must be handled appropriately.

> Being psychosomatic does not make their concerns any less real, or any less important.
>
> Camilo Jorge

The job for a provider is to determine what the condition really is and how best to manage it.

> Some patients cannot be treated solely by medications, but instead have to be treated with psychology, with diplomacy.
>
> Camilo Jorge

The concern expressed by these providers is that if not properly managed, a person with these types of conditions will return repeatedly.

> The physician has to know how to work his way through the psycho-somatic problems to get to the medical ones.
>
> Camilo Jorge

A second type of problem is when strong emotions trigger another condition. For example, in 1998, Los Angeles–based Latino patients in a diabetes study by the Center for the Study of Latino Health and Culture (CESLAC) perceived the onset of diabetes as the result of heredity, improper diet, being over-weight, a lack of exercise, and *susto*, a Latino folk illness.

> I have heard that diabetes is caused by an angry personality (bilis), or a strong fright (susto), or even a strong desire for something.
>
> Patient focus group member

But not all Latino medical behavior has its source in the emotions. Latino and non-Hispanic white nonimmunized elderly voiced very different concerns in one study (CDC 1997). Non-Hispanic elderly expressed little desire to be immunized, did not trust immunizations, and did not believe they were useful. Latino elderly, on the other hand, expressed a great desire to be immunized. Their concerns were not emotional but logistical: where to get an immunization, how to pay for it, and how to arrange for transportation to a medical facility.

ALTERNATIVE HEALING PRACTICES

Non-Latino providers may be most familiar with, and puzzled by, Latino patients' advocacy of alternative healing practices. Yet Latino providers take the existence of these practices for granted. The question is how to manage the health of a patient, knowing that additional healing styles may be used.

> Often, they [patients] have consulted an herbalist, a chiropractor, and a local pharmacist.
>
> Mercedes Brenneisen-Goode

Healers

There are many alternative healers that a Latino patient might use: *curandera, sobador, huesero, yerbero, espiritista*. Latino or culturally competent providers feel no reticence in asking patients if they are seeing another type of healer, so that the provider may take that into account.

> Because of my attitude, patients don't hide from me the fact that they are seeing *curanderas*.
>
> Camilo Jorge

Herbal Cures

In addition to over-the-counter nostra available in any drugstore or health store, Latino patients often resort to a wide variety of herbal cures. Latino providers had varying opinions about their utility (some approved, others disapproved), but all agreed that it was important to know what other medications a patient was taking. They further agreed that it was important to incorporate such knowledge in ways that were not distasteful for the patient.

> Many of my patients use herbal remedies. Personally, I do not accept such use, but neither do I deny it.... I would never say, "Stop using those herbal remedies."
>
> Camilo Jorge

Rather, the successful approach is to use herbal remedies as a way of opening up discussion about using medicines in general.

> I told him, simply, "Señor, these herbs may feel good, but they will do nothing to get rid of that [kidney] stone. Let's see if we can find a way to take care of it."
>
> Camilo Jorge

BELIEFS

Latino medical and healing beliefs have often been trivialized as "folk beliefs" about illness and health. Latino providers see these beliefs as something more profound, as a cultural pattern that helps Latinos to make sense of the world. Beyond the folk illnesses mentioned by the providers, some other important beliefs surfaced.

Organs and Spirit

Needing an organ transplant can highlight specific Latino beliefs about the relation between organs, the body, and the spirit. These beliefs must be understood to enable surgical practice.

> The Latino patient believes that character—kindness or meanness, astuteness, love and passion—comes from the heart.
>
> Ismael Navarro Nuño

This belief actually has Aztec antecedents. As early as 1535, Bernardo de Sahagún, a Franciscan priest who was among the first Europeans to study Aztec culture, mentioned the Aztec belief in the heart as the seat of the soul. As we enter the twenty-first century, Latino patients continue this view of the human being.

> When I counsel patients for possible heart transplant, their concern is not survival, but rather, whose soul will live inside of them.
>
> Ismael Navarro Nuño

The importance of the heart as the physical source of character produces a specific concern in Latino patients who need heart transplants. Though they may understand the technology of a heart transplant, the fear of radical personality change following the operation is a vivid one.

> Once the old and diseased heart of the patient is removed, these patients believe, the soul will also be lost.
>
> Ismael Navarro Nuño

Then, once a new heart is introduced,

> What happens, then, to a patient who receives a heart transplant? Will his character change? Will Jovita lose her kindheartedness?
>
> Ismael Navarro Nuño

The provider must address and settle these philosophical issues for the patient's peace of mind, who might believe that

> a totally new individual will emerge. So should we mourn the symbolic death of the patient at the time of the transplant?
>
> Ismael Navarro Nuño

Modesty
Latino providers often mention the importance of modesty to their patients.

> At times, I have come across Latino patients who would rather die of their heart disease than give up their modesty.
>
> Ismael Navarro Nuño

Familiarity with the cultural importance of modesty allows providers to negotiate the issue properly.

> The mother of a teenage Mexican girl I was about to operate on requested very emotionally that she be allowed to stay with her daughter day and night—including going to the operating room—so that she might make sure her daughter's body was not seen naked by male doctors and nurses.
>
> Ismael Navarro Nuño

The mother's concern was taken seriously; she was reassured that there would always be female nurses in attendance.

Family

The research of Marín et al. (1990) in smoking cessation has shown that Latinos and non-Latinos respond to different prevention "triggers." Generally, non-Latinos stop smoking based on appeals to individual health. The message that smoking is "bad for you," a focus on the damage smoking causes, and a generally unglamorous image for smokers will often persuade a white non-Latino to consider smoking cessation. Such individualizing messages generally do not produce a similar response in Latinos. Instead, Latinos respond to the family-oriented message that smoking is bad for their family, especially children.

Becoming Culturally Competent

The purpose of this book is to enable interested providers in communicating with their non-Latino colleagues about cultural effectiveness. It is important that non-Latinos learn to be effective since a study showed that in 1999 only 4.8 percent of physicians licensed to practice in California were Latino (Hayes-Bautista et al. 1999). In comparison, the Latino population in California is about 40 percent of the total population. To put this another way, for every non-Latino physician in California, there are 335 non-Latino Californians, but for every Latino physician in the state, there are 2,893 Latino Californians. Obviously, the need for culturally competent doctors far outstrips the number of Latino doctors currently practicing. While increasing the number of Latino doctors is essential, increasing all doctors' cultural competency is important as well. Until the Latino physician shortage is filled, non-Latino physicians will have to learn culturally effective ways of providing medical care services.

The premise of this book is that cultural competence is a learned skill, within the reach of any practitioner. Cultural competence does not come without effort, however; as with any skill, it requires an investment of time and effort. The providers writing in this book have underscored several important areas that need to be mastered by all providers interested in becoming culturally competent in healing Latinos. In particular it is important to understand indirect patterns of communication, the role of emotions in Latinos' perception of illness, and beliefs in alternative healing practices, the intersection of body and spirit, and modesty.

Communication between the patient and provider is facilitated when both can speak the same language. Good patient relations are most easily built when language is not a barrier to communication. Language acquisition is time consuming and requires constant effort. However, the rewards are well worth the effort.

> I can only beam with pride when I hear my non-Latino colleagues doing their best to speak Spanish to their patients, for I know that they truly care about them.
>
> Arturo Velazquez Jr.

Some medical schools now offer medical Spanish, and there are any number of opportunities to study Spanish through university extension courses, community colleges, and private organizations.

Understanding patients' cultural patterns leads to more meaningful interaction. As may be surmised from these brief examples, Latino patients have mental constructs of health and illness that are very different from those of non-Hispanics. As Latino patients come to represent a larger proportion of a medical group's enrollee base, it becomes more important to understand these mental constructs. Cultural competency shows practitioners the keys to motivating patients to become involved in their own health care and thus is a critical component in the brave new world of twenty-first-century medicine. Yet, much of the training in cultural competence consists of well-intended lists that nevertheless do not address sources of behavior. The providers writing in this book did not study Latino cultural competency—they lived it. And that, perhaps, is the best way for anyone—Latino or non-Latino—to acquire cultural understanding. It need not require living abroad.

> To understand the Mexican American, take the time to go into the barrios....By befriending members of the community,...learn to become culturally sensitive to their needs.
>
> Arturo Velazquez Jr.

By working in Latino settings with an open mind, any provider's knowledge base can be expanded.

Works Cited

CDC (Centers for Disease Control and Prevention). 1997. "Vaccination Levels among Hispanics and Non-Hispanic Whites Aged (greater than or equal to) 65 years—Los Angeles County, California, 1996." *Morbidity and Mortality Weekly Report* 46, no. 49 (December 12): 1165–68.

Glaser, Barney, and Anselm Strauss. 1967. *The Discovery of Grounded Theory*. Chicago: Aldine.

Hayes-Bautista, David E. 2004. *La Nueva California: Latinos in the Golden State*. Berkeley: University of California Press.

Hayes-Bautista, David E., Paul Hsu, Robert Beltran, and Juan Villagomez. 1999. *The Latino Physician Shortage in California*. Los Angeles: Center for the Study of Latino Health and Culture, Division of General Internal Medicine and Health Services Research, UCLA School of Medicine.

Hurtado, Aida, David E. Hayes-Bautista, R. Burciaga Valdez, and Anthony Hernandez. 1992. *Redefining California: Latino Social Participation in Multicultural Society*. UCLA: Chicano Studies Research Center.

Marín, Barbara V., Gerardo Marín, Regina Otero-Sabogal, Fabio Sabogal, and Eliseo J. Pérez-Stable. 1990. *Cultural Differences in Attitudes toward Smoking: Developing Messages Using the Theory of Reasoned Action*. San Francisco: UCSF Hispanic Smoking Cessation Project.

Dolor de Cabeza
Headache—Depression or Martyrdom?

Felipe O. Santana

*I*n 1993, I closed a successful private practice of fourteen years to work part-time as a psychologist at Clinicas del Camino Real, a comprehensive health services clinic for the poor, especially Latinos, in Oxnard, California. The clinic, one of six in Ventura County, serves a city with 153,000 inhabitants, with an additional 60,000 migrants, seasonal and permanent, living there. Ninety-one percent of patient encounters at the Oxnard clinic are with patients whose yearly income averages $200 below the federal poverty level.

I vividly remember the first two weeks I worked at Clinicas. My patients' major complaints were headaches, "like if something is squeezing the back of my head," patient after patient explained. I initially suspected that most of these patients had migraine headaches, because they also had symptoms such as nausea and other stomach problems. But I felt I was in an awkward position. A voice inside my head kept saying, "They don't have any emotional problems. They need to see a medical doctor, not me." But these patients had been referred to me by the physicians in the clinic's medical department. How could I send them back unless the MDs were wrong?

But while listening to a patient during my second week at the clinic, a light went on inside my head. "*Idiota*," I said. "How dumb can you be?" With a flash of insight, I understood what I had been seeing. The problem was not with the patients—it was with me. I had worked for so many years with the well-to-do and the well-schooled that I had forgotten my own roots, my own culture. Clear in my mind came my mother's words: "*Si el hambre de dobla, que la dignidad te enderezca*" (If hunger bends you, may your pride straighten you).

Born very poor in Isla de Pinos, Cuba, I grew up feeling the socioeconomic discrimination that exists in Latin countries. In Havana, the capital, that feeling was almost asphyxiating. My father was a longshoreman and my mother a housewife. Both of my parents were almost illiterate, but they embedded three principles in me: a work ethic, a hunger to know, and an ambition to progress. My father, who was one of the most brilliant men I know, encouraged me to challenge ideas and to investigate my own truth. Accepted on scholarship at a residential private school, I began to work toward a degree in psychology. I worked as a servant for the other students and the dormitory master seven days a week. On vacations, I worked as a construction worker, in packinghouses, or as a longshoreman. My income helped out my family and bought school materials for the upcoming semester. Finally, I earned a doctoral degree in psychology from the University of Havana.

My father's philosophy sustained me as a political refugee in the United States. I came to California, went to UCLA, got the units that I needed to revalidate my degree, and began doing research at UCLA on schizophrenia, the prevention of drug addiction in children, and epidemiological research on mental illness in the United States. At the same time, I was working as director of the Pacoima–San Fernando–Arleta clinic of the Golden State Community Mental Health Center, serving a low-income neighborhood in the San Fernando Valley. From there I went to Ventura County, forty-five miles northwest of Los Angeles, working first as senior psychologist and finally retiring as senior program administrator for the county's Department of Alcohol and Drug Programs.

In that second week at Clinicas, the experiences of my American professional life fell away, and I returned to my roots. Everything became clear to me. Everything made sense. I was present with my patients. I began to utilize the appropriate cultural tools. I did not need to begin by asking questions. I did not need to be systematic. I was able to learn what I needed through a conversation, during which almost all the information was revealed without my prompting. This method, developed through my experience, was both profound and simple.

Assessment—in any culture—begins in the waiting room. Who is sitting next to whom? Where is the person sitting? What does their body language convey? Instead of showing them the way to my office, I began to be informal with my Latino patients, trying to relax them, asking questions like "How is the weather outside?" I would ask these poor, unschooled Latinos where they would like to sit, thus validating their importance. If they didn't want to sit down at first, I would say, "Please, you are my guest. Sit down." Then they would sit.

Next, I would normally pose the question "Where do you come from?" After the patient answered, I might respond, "Oh, I have been there" (if I truly had) or "I know some people from that region," and give some more information about the subject, or "I don't know anything about that region." The well-to-do and school-educated consider this method a waste of their time, and time is money. But with the Latino culture on which we are focusing, these questions mean "I care"; this personal approach has a great value.

When I have some knowledge about the patient's home region, I give some input, then I request validation from the patient about my knowledge. If I don't have any information, I request it (this disrupts the hierarchy between us, making the patient "the expert"). From what they tell me, I can determine whether they are from a rural or an urban location. At this point, I would follow with, "Is all of your family from that area?" This will provide an idea of the family constellation. If I do not get enough information, I will ask, "Are you the oldest or youngest in your family? How many brothers or sisters?" I like to ask, "Was there a plaza in your town?" In 95 percent of Latin American towns and cities, there is a plaza where the city hall, elementary school, and Catholic Church are located. This provides a way to assess religious background. "Were there usually a lot of children playing in the area?" The answer to this question would give me socioeconomic information. If they did not play after a certain age, was it due to a lack of toys, need to help out in the home, school attendance, or a job?

Along with these questions, the therapist can interject personal experiences of early childhood (though this may not be acceptable in some theoretical orientations) as well as some funny memories or jokes. Latinos love to make jokes, even when they are under stress, as a release for repressed, painful feelings. The rhythm and timing of the conversation is dictated by the patient, not the therapist. By this time, the patient usually feels at home and will have provided the therapist with a background on the family, social status, religious upbringing, and birth order in a brief assessment session.

From the patient's point of view, the first real "doctor–patient" question comes when I ask, "How do you come to be in my office today?" The patient may respond, "Well, Dr. So-and-so told me to come," or "A friend of mine told me about you." After this statement, something changes. Sometimes the therapist can hear the confusion between *doctor* and *padre* (Catholic priest). This is one of the many differences between a school-educated patient and a poor, less formally educated one.

Religion is a very powerful force in the lives of Latino patients. The majority of this population are Catholic or evangelical Christians (I notice more and more Latinos are becoming evangelical Christians). Particularly with the Catholics, the respect for the priest, whom they consider sacred and to whom, when they confess, they entrust their deepest confidences, is profound. It is not difficult to understand that in the patient's mind, there is a strong association between priest and therapist, because the therapist is also bound by confidentiality. But their religion does not entirely explain the Latino patient's confusion of doctor and priest. The poor in Latino culture have been dominated for generations by the powerful in their homeland; people learned to obey orders for survival. Respect for all figures of authority is natural. When they come to the United States, the situation continues and if they become dependent on the social system—a system they may not fully understand—the hierarchy is even more controlling. But the doctor–priest association allows the Latino to talk to a therapist about the most intimate thoughts.

Assessment of the case is done indirectly, again in a conversational fashion. The patient might say, "The doctor referred me to you. I have very strong headaches in the back of my head and sometimes I have stomach problems." My question is, "Then the doctor knows what is going on?" "Well, they think that it is my nerves." Not that they are depressed or anxious, but it is the patient's "nerves." Now the assessment begins to focus on the pathology. Often the patient begins to cry at this point and

I may comment, *"Parece que está muy triste"* (It seems to me you are very sad). The typical answer is, "You don't know how many problems I have."

María, forty-seven, born on a ranch in Mexico, came to the United States six years ago. Her husband had come to the United States before her, and every year he went back to Mexico to visit his wife and the children. When María finally arrived in the United States, she became pregnant. Now she had four children—the oldest seventeen, the youngest five. When she arrived here, people began to tell her how unfaithful her husband had been while he was living here without her. María didn't want to pay attention, telling herself it was just gossip. When she came to see me, she told me about the headaches but talked about how many problems she had. As a therapist, I needed to interpret the patient's words, but I had to listen without interrupting. Later I could ask for clarification.

The story began to unfold. "I found that he was doing something he wasn't supposed to do. It happened one day when we went to a party. At home, we began putting the kids to bed. When we undressed, I noticed something, so I asked him. Then he said that yes, it was something on the street, and I know how men are, and he didn't know what had come over him."

As you can see, she did not give much information, merely a lot of innuendo, and even this was difficult for the patient to express verbally. But she kept on talking, giving me information and data.

"He came and hugged me one day and I noticed two papers inside of his shirt. He took off his shirt and there were two sales tickets for shoes for kids about four years of age. I confronted him, and he said that he didn't know what it was all about. He said that maybe the sales slips were in his van, which he uses to transport kids to soccer games, and maybe that is where they came from."

After she explained the story her way, I slowly began to probe. I asked two direct questions, but indirectly, opening the door for more specific answers from her. "Well, you mentioned that you found something on him when he undressed. Did you find some men's juices in his pants?" The patient answered, "No, no, no, it was not that. I found a hickey in the middle of his chest. I knew that I didn't do that, because I don't do that." Then she was more explicit about the rest of the situation. She had overheard a telephone conversation in which her husband told his mistress, the mother of four-year-old twins, how much he loved her. María then visited the store where her husband had bought one pair of shoes, on a day he claimed he was going to Immigration. The clerk remembered sending him to another store to get the matching pair. By now, she was describing her confrontations with her husband, which are still occurring, and she asked me what she should do.

I explained to María that I was going to help her clear her mind, but that she would have to make her own decision, because it was her life. I added that I would be more than happy to help her find the answers she needed, but that I believed she already had the answers. She looked at me and smiled. It was then that the therapeutic bonding took effect, and she then began the process of separating from him. She had a meeting with the children, explaining to them what they undoubtedly already knew; they understood and still respected their mother. The husband refused to come to marriage counseling. I am currently working on this case.

How did this woman come to see me? Very simple. She went to see her medical doctor because she had headaches and pain in the back of her neck, and she felt like her head was going to explode. Her physician, after doing a series of tests, found there was nothing physically wrong with her, so he referred her to me. I began her case with the premise that she had a headache and a note from her personal physician stating she might be depressed. Based on my personal experiences, I inferred that the headaches were caused by the unconscious searching for an acceptable way to discuss personal problems with a stranger.

In the Latino culture, particularly in the poorly educated group that I work with, people do not go out of their family circle to talk about their problems. Usually there is a family member designated to be the "surrogate therapist" to whom family members will go first. If no one in the family has this role, they will go to the mother, followed by the extended family. Secondly, they talk to the priest. Then, when they try and all the doors are closed, unconsciously they know they have to seek professional help. If they go to a psychologist, a psychiatrist, or a mental health professional, they and their circle will think they are "crazy." But if they get a headache, they will go to their physician, and the physician may then refer the patient to a mental health practitioner. That way is more acceptable, because the physician is the one who made the referral.

In Latino culture, teachers, priests, and medical doctors wield a tremendous amount of power. In such a structure, individuals usually (and remember there are exceptions to every rule) believe what the well-schooled say. If a medical doctor made the referral, the patient now has a kind of permission to talk freely to a psychotherapist. If the family finds out, it is accepted, because "poor Mrs. X has so many problems with that husband of hers," or "with her children," or "with other family members." Less-educated Latino patients usually come to a mental health professional through such a referral.

Something else we must remember is that the mothers rule the Latino household; it is, in effect, a matriarchal society. The fathers may perhaps scream, yell, and abuse—although there are cases where the mother does that, too—but the mother is in charge. If the father is the king, the mother is the prime minister. When something happens with the children, it is *her* responsibility. When something is lacking in the house, it is *her* responsibility. The father, in most cases, represents strength, but the mother is the power: "*Padre puede ser qualquiera, pero madre hay una sola*" (The father could be anyone, but mother—only one).

Veneration of the mother certainly has its source in the beliefs of the Catholic Church. The Virgin Mary, called by different names in different countries, is the symbol of divinity on earth. As described in the New Testament of the Bible, the Greek word *agape*—to love something above us, bigger than us—describes human love for God. For the Latin Catholic, giving love to the Virgin Mary—the mother of all mothers—is *agape* love. In the Latin culture, that *agape* is expected by both church and society to be given to earthly mothers as well, but on a smaller scale. The love for a father is *philia*, a Greek word that describes love for someone at one's own level. I have noticed that love for the father is never as great as that for the mother. The father is more respected due to fear, which the mother also instills in the children. This religious societal structure gives the mother extreme power in the majority of cases.

Recently, there has been a strong move by the evangelical Protestant religions to proselytize Latinos from Latin America who come to the United States. These evangelical Protestants have one thing in common with Catholics: guilt is a very strong component of both religions. A person needs to suffer, and part of the suffering, especially for Catholics, has to involve physical or emotional pain. Pain will redeem. Suffering will take us up to heaven. Suffering through pain creates martyrs—and how are you going to attack a martyr? Martyrdom can be an effective way of controlling the environment, including the people in it. People without control unconsciously discover that martyrdom can confer upon them the power they crave.

When the husband puts pressure on his wife, or takes over her domain by putting emotional or physical pressure on her, she may say yes to placate him. Then the passive-aggressive resistance begins, which may result in the woman having a lot of headaches. The wife becomes a martyr. At this point, she needs the care and solicitation of everyone around her. That is the way she regains her control in the house. It is a very powerful tool. That is the etiology of most of these headaches. When poor Latinos come to me for therapy, I know I am not dealing with headaches that are related to any type of chemical imbalance or organicity.

When asking if a patient is depressed, I follow up with a specific question, even if the patient now knows that the question is meant to elicit specific symptoms. It is cross-cultural—it does not matter which ethnic group, which socioeconomic group, which social group the individual is associated with. If depression is involved, the patient may become anhedonic or anergic, experience sleeping problems, suffer weight gain or loss. If I suspect a patient is depressed or clinically depressed, my therapy will differ for upper-middle-class, school-educated Latinos and non-Latinos.

With the less-educated population, the first therapeutic point to consider is the hierarchy. The patient expects the doctor to advise what to do. Does that mean that he will do it? Not necessarily. The patient wants to hear my opinion, wants me to advise, even though he may still do as he pleases. As therapists, we know that telling the patient what to do is unacceptable, regardless of what ethnicity or socioeconomic level we're dealing with. I will provide therapy as I always do, up to a point, which I will explain further as we go along. More alternatives will be explored, influenced by cognitive milieu, allowing the exploration of different alternatives and allowing the patient to find solutions, especially if I assess that they are in the "flutter" stage. If a patient is in that stage, my red flags will rise; this type of Latino patient wants solutions right now, during their crisis stage. I will add problem solving, using a lot of analogies, vignettes, stories, and anecdotes, which will make the patient think and help in decision making.

The therapy has to be structured without a structure: you know that you are going to be jumping from one place to the other, but you structure it so that you jump in an orderly fashion. Sometimes you are going to be talking about family things, then what happened with the neighbors, then what happened to the dog. You have to give the time, and in therapy, timing is a key element. Ethnicity or socioeconomics makes no difference; in the Latino culture, timing is imperative, not a therapist's choice. If the therapist is not accustomed to this type of culture and loses timing, the therapist will lose credibility. The patient will believe the doctor does not understand. The patient will be lost.

When working with the poor and unschooled Latino patients, the hierarchical culture of this population comes into play. Religion has a very strong influence and needs to be used as an ally, with full respect accorded to their faith. There is an underlying power struggle in which the mother maintains control by victimizing herself (becoming a martyr) and the father by imposing his will on the family, while being largely absent in the upbringing of the children. It is of the utmost importance to keep both parents' pride intact. Remember that pride is one of the few possessions they have, and great respect for that pride is mandatory. The point is to bring the mother and the father together.

Poor, informally educated Latinos express distress through headaches: look for depression, anxiety, or martyrdom and apply the conversational assessment accordingly. Indirect therapy—with cognitive, behavioral, and didactic therapy tinting the treatment—helps, as well as using humor when appropriate. If a patient comes directly to you with no referral, with headaches, refer the patient to a medical doctor in order to eliminate any physical problems (which any good therapist would do anyway). If the physical aspect is eliminated, then begin conversational assessment for depression, anxiety, or martyrdom.

Each patient, even with the same diagnosis, exhibits his or her pathology in a unique way and needs to be treated accordingly. Modalities of treatment must be developed to fit the patient's needs, not to "plug" the patient into the theoretical orientations the therapist is inclined to use.

Mexican or Mexican American?

Arturo Velazquez Jr.

*I*magine yourself as a physician fresh out of medical school, out to change the world. Imagine yourself in a small town in Mexico, armed only with a medical bag containing the usual instruments: stethoscope, otoscope/ophthalmoscope, measuring tape, reflex hammer, tuning fork, safety pins, blood pressure cuff, tongue depressors, maybe a thermometer or two. Imagine yourself having to see patients with no access to a sophisticated lab or X-ray unit. Imagine working with only a few dozen medications to fall back on, most of them samples provided by pharmaceutical representatives or donated by the local health department. Could you work under those conditions? Would you?

If you were a graduate of a Mexican medical school, you would—or you would never receive your formal degree. The all-important sixth year is a year of social service or community service demanded of all graduates in the health care professions. Here you find out what the real world is like: how to practice medicine on a shoestring (sometimes that is all you have to tie a knot in a baby's umbilical cord). You learn to use all your training—and your guile—to make your patients better, or keep them from getting worse. Your first call might teach you to administer intravenous fluids hung from a nail fastened to a wall made of sticks, air blowing in between them. The IV replenishes the vital fluids and electrolytes your patient lost due to persistent vomiting and diarrhea. As you sit before an open hearth on a wooden chair nestled on hard-packed earth, you sip strong black coffee, eat tortillas and beans with chili, which the mother has scrounged up from somewhere to offer you in payment for your services. After the patient improves, you see the look of profound gratitude in the family's eyes and wonder if you were overpaid. And you think back on all the hours you spent in training, wondering if anything you would ever do for a patient could make a difference. Suddenly, you realize that you can make a difference if you want to, and with this realization, you have taken the initial steps in your life-long calling.

Imagine yourself looking into the bloodshot eyes of a nine-year-old girl who has been bitten by a rattlesnake. After cleaning her red, swollen leg, you give her an antibiotic shot, get her started on intravenous antivenin, and send her by ambulance to the nearest hospital, forty miles away. Only later would you discover, in frustration, that the vial of antivenin you administered was the only one available in the entire county; unless she gets the necessary five more vials soon, she will never see her tenth birthday.

Imagine yourself recommending herbal teas and poultices for sores, colds, and coughs because no medicines are available, and because that is all the patient can afford. Imagine yourself setting fractures with wood planks or rolled-up newspaper as casting materials.

Imagine yourself diagnosing pneumonia based on clinical signs and symptoms only, not knowing for sure how sick your patient is. Imagine praying to God that the injection you gave would help, because no transportation was available to the nearest hospital, since all ambulances were transporting the victims of a head-on collision of two buses in dense fog.

The best recommendation I can make to the altruistic physician who wants to learn to treat Latino patients with cultural sensitivity and competence is to spend a month or two in such a small Mexican town, clinging to the coattails of the local doctor or the doctor doing a year of community service. Tag along, look into the eyes of the children and worried parents, and try to reassure them that their child will be fine, wondering meanwhile if the child has bronchitis or pneumonia.

Go to the town church after Mass and watch the townsfolk pray on bended knees before the Virgin of Guadalupe, or Saint Anthony of Padua, or Saint Martin de Porres to heal the sick, as they make offerings of gold medals in the form of legs or arms or heads, representing the particular area that needs to be cured. Such an immersion is the ideal way to learn how to be culturally and medically sensitive to the needs of the Mexican immigrant in the United States.

To understand the Mexican American, take the time to go into the barrios, found anywhere a significant number of Mexican Americans live. On the surface, you see a constellation of individuals who may be fluent in English, are hardworking, and often interact with their coworkers as any American in our society would. But the Mexican heritage runs deep in these individuals. They see themselves as part of a larger, but often ignored, subgroup. Some of their health needs are a product of their living standards in the United States. Other illnesses are the product of a distinctive diet or of genetic susceptibility handed down through their Mexican ancestors. Their religion, for the most part Catholic, plays a significant role in how they will respond to illness. The exposure to folk medicine, handed down from family members, also may play a role in access to timely health care.

Non-Latino doctors might do volunteer work in community centers and free clinics. By befriending members of the community, volunteers might earn invitations into their patients' homes and thereby learn to become culturally sensitive to their needs. This is no easy task. It is difficult for an outsider to learn in a few weeks or months a different language and culture that others have had the benefit of understanding from the day they were born. But such sensitivity is possible for the truly dedicated doctor. I can only beam with pride when I hear my non-Latino colleagues doing their best to speak Spanish to their patients, for I know that they truly care about them.

One step on the road toward understanding the Latino patient involves distinguishing those born abroad and those born in the United States. I define a Mexican as a citizen of Mexico, usually a person born and raised there, usually Spanish speaking but possibly a speaker of a number of Indian languages native to Mexico. In the United States, a Mexican immigrant may speak English with varying degrees of fluency, but almost always with a mild to heavy accent. In their approach to health care, recent arrivals are very traditional, almost submissive in their attitudes, and usually very grateful to their physicians. In Mexico, the two most respected vocations are medicine and the priesthood. Catholics—and for the most part Mexican immigrants are Catholic—often accept their illnesses as punishment from God and ask the Virgin Mary to intercede on their behalf to make them healthy again. Their main hope in seeing a physician is to get a shot of penicillin or some other medication so they can get back to work quickly, to provide for their immediate family and often for those left behind in Mexico.

This desire for a quick cure is prevalent not only among the poor but also among the better-educated of the newcomers and is readily witnessed throughout Mexico.

A Mexican American is a person born in the United States or brought here young enough so that he considers himself American. U.S. citizenship is usually a defining trait, but again, heritage is rooted in Mexico and its traditions. Mexican Americans may speak English fluently if well educated, but if of the lower socioeconomic class, may have fair to poor English skills. Mexican Americans will also have varying degrees of Spanish fluency, and their Spanish may be affected by a barrio accent or dialect.

Frequently, only others of Mexican descent can distinguish Mexican Americans from native Mexicans. There are differences in dress and language usage. Mexican Americans tend to be less formal in their appearance; some will more readily put tattoos on the body to commemorate a loved one or display member-ship in a street gang.

Though most Mexican Americans are Catholics and as such may accept illness as a punishment from God, they may also blame others, or the system, for their ills. As a general rule, they are less likely to ask the Virgin's help in their cure.

Most Mexican Americans have lost their submissiveness in regards to health care and view it as a right. Educated in the United States, they are often more vocal and assertive in seek-ing out what they perceive to be the best care for them. A few are even rude and disrespectful to physicians in general; some use threats of litigation and frequent complaints to get themselves better treatment, whether they are entitled to the service or not.

In my experience, second and later generations of Mexican Americans usually don't see themselves as anything other than full Americans. They take great pride in being Americans and see Mexico as the land of their ancestors but a place totally foreign to them. They are usually English dominant and have at least a high school education. They are conscious of their rights and have high expectations in regard to all aspects of life, especially health care. Usually they have learned to be quite polite in their dealings with physicians and have thought out their course of action if their needs are not met; they are the ones who usually effect change within the system when they are dissatisfied with something. Some have the patience to work through and with the system to their advantage, with a high tendency to seek legal recourse, if necessary.

Among Mexican Americans, some view Mexicans as outsiders and have a very vocal "foreigner go home" attitude. I once had a second- or third-generation Mexican American patient who had developed palpitations as the result of cocaine use the previous day. She was brought to the clinic by her older sister, and before I had an opportunity to question the patient, the sister was already complaining bitterly about the medical assistant's incompetence. Apparently he had spoken to her in heavily accented English, asking a few background questions. The sister had to repeat herself several times, as the medical assistant did not fully understand her. Medical assistants should be fluent in English before even being considered for a job, she complained. In her view, imperfect English equaled incompetence, and this immigrant should go back to where he came from. She was terribly incensed by this lack of "professionalism" on the part of the medical assistant. Although the assistant had done nothing wrong, the sister's anger over him ultimately affected her relation with me. The patient and her sister ended up leaving the clinic to seek treatment elsewhere, where there were "real nurses" who spoke English. I have often had to deal with similar situations, but usually I am more successful in directing the conversation away from the assistants to focus on the patient's physical problem. Medical professionals planning to work with the Latino community should realize that there are such tensions between Mexicans and Mexican Americans.

I can usually tell if I am dealing with a Mexican American or a Mexican through their dress. Mexican Americans of the lower socioeconomic class often have tattoos, beards, and goatees; wear their hair slicked back, long and unkempt or very short; and may dress in the oversized pants, sneakers, and other attire of teenage, gang-influenced fashion. The women may wear very tight, short blouses with pants or miniskirts, and not infrequently sport tattoos. Many use heavy makeup but have plucked out most of their eyebrows. The tendency to obesity in both sexes is noticeable, even in childhood. Better-educated Mexican Americans (many are college graduates) usually dress more conservatively, though some may have the tattoos that have now become a fad among even middle-class Americans. A concern for controlling their weight seems to prevail. When I hear them speaking in the waiting or examination rooms, I have some idea of what language to speak with them, even before the first introductions.

Mexicans run the full gamut, from illiterate to university graduates. Their manner of dress is usually subdued, with a tendency to favor blue jeans and boots, western-style hats, and a well-trimmed moustache if one is worn. Business suits and dress shoes become more frequent as the population leaves blue-collar jobs for the service industry. The hair is cut medium to short, and their overall demeanor remains more modest than that of their Mexican American brethren. Mexican women appear in house dresses, though pants and blouses, when worn, are not as revealing as those worn by their Mexican American sisters; hair may be long or short, but is not overly stylish, and makeup is sparingly used, giving the women a more natural look. Hair coloring is uncommon. The trend toward obesity is not as noticeable in younger Mexican natives, and morbid obesity is less prevalent than in Mexican Americans, even in the older immigrants.

At our first meeting, I may start with a simple *buenos dias* or hello and then ask the nature of the visit. Usually, the Spanish-dominant patient will politely ask me to speak Spanish. Those who are bilingual usually do not mind which language I use. Others will state the language they prefer. On the other hand, if the patient is English-speaking only, it can be the equivalent of a slap in the face if I don't speak English right off. Later generations generally are a bit embarrassed that they don't speak Spanish and often lament their inability to speak their ancestral language. Despite my experience in the Latino community, I sometimes unintentionally offend some patients.

Once I get beyond the initial introductions and learn the reason for their visit, if I am conversing with a Mexican national, I may ask about his or her wearing apparel, especially if it appears Mexican-made. Hats, belts, dresses or blouses, and some leather jackets show distinctive features, which can give clues to regional origin. Jewelry, especially silver, for which Mexico is known, may also serve as a conversation piece and help put the patient at ease with the physician. Even the way Spanish is spoken can give clues to the country of origin. The accents and idiosyncrasies of the language can be quite pronounced, not only among Mexicans and Mexican Americans but also among the natives of Central and South America. I find that my knowledge of and firsthand experience with Mexican customs, national and religious holidays, and Mexico's political, educational, and health care systems help me in many cases to break the ice and form a common bond.

Quite often the patients will want to know where I am from, and at that point I make it a sort of game for them and myself. Most are surprised when I tell them that I am not a Mexican citizen, but appear relieved when I explain that my parents are from Mexico, that I have spent a good part of my life in Mexico, and that my wife is from Mexico. Invariably, they are interested about how a non-Mexican could know so much about Mexico and Mexicans. For me to claim to be a Mexican would be offensive to many, as I painfully discovered when, as a teenager, I was called a traitor to my race because I had been born in the United States. But by showing ample respect for Mexico and affirming my Mexican roots, the respect and loyalty of the patients can be earned.

Over the years, I have discovered that accepting myself as "not quite Mexican" has in some ways helped Mexicans identify with me. The fact that my medical school training, including an internship and social service, was in Mexico itself has made the transition smoother than it might otherwise have been. My fluency in both English and Spanish allows me to form a much-needed bridge between the predominantly Spanish-speaking community that I proudly serve and the American medical establishment and its confusing array of technology, services, and resources. I have gained a measure of status and credibility with my success as a physician, which reassures my patients that I won't let them down. Trust has been a key factor in my credibility as a physician, especially among Mexicans and many first-generation Mexican Americans.

Still, it can be more difficult to gain the trust of lower socio-economic Mexican American patients, especially the women. They may feel that I am not a good doctor if I utter the "shot" word in front of their children. Mexican Americans as a general rule don't like to receive intramuscular injections, and, in the American health system, the trend is away from injections. But most Mexicans prefer to get a shot so that they can get better sooner, a custom prevalent in most Latin American countries.

For the most part, Mexicans would like to speak to their physician without a third party translating and thus becoming aware of some potentially embarrassing information. This is understand-able. For them, visiting a doctor is like going to confession; it is appropriate for the parishioner and the priest and not anyone else. A Spanish-speaking physician allows the patient to be candid and have a reasonable expectation of having one's medical needs met. Non-Spanish-speaking physicians may tend to cut the patient visit short or fail to understand the gravity of the patient's complaints. I find myself spending quite a bit of time with my first-time patients, even if the consultation is for a limited problem. I try to impress upon them that I take their problems seriously and reassure them that I will do everything in my power to help. But I also request my patients' compliance with treatment recommendations—or a very good reason for noncompliance. For instance, with my cash-paying patients, I insist they let me know if they can afford to purchase their medications. If they can't buy the medicine, the prescription is worthless paper and a waste of my time and theirs. I will sometimes waive my fee to allow the patients to buy the needed medicines. At times, I can help with samples to give them a head start on the treatment until payday comes around. Quite often, I find myself using the most inexpensive medicine that will do the job, almost without thinking. If I have to use a more expensive medication, I usually let the patient know why I recommend it in spite of the cost. I sometimes am forced to remind noncompliant patients that I have a working arrangement with God: "I don't do miracles and He doesn't practice medicine."

I had a female patient come to me for a persistent urinary tract infection, which had lasted approximately a month and a half, previously treated by one white and three Asian doctors. She spoke only Spanish and none of her doctors did. She wanted me to cure her right away, but when I asked what medications she had been on, she became rather annoyed and said, "I left them at home. You are the doctor and you are supposed to know how to cure me. I don't know what medicines you doctors prescribe." I had the patient return home and bring in all the medicines she was taking. She brought back four empty bottles of Bactrim from four different doctors. I sent this patient's urine out for a culture and, using the information gleaned from her, I put her on a trial of Macrodantin. Seventy-two hours later, the lab reported that the culture grew *E. coli* resistant to Bactrim but sensitive to Macrodantin. By then, my patient was much better and, of course, very grateful for the relief obtained from her urinary tract infection. I could easily have made the same mistake as my previous colleagues did if I had not taken the time to investigate her complaint fully.

I recall a Mexican patient who used an ointment to treat a flea bite. He subsequently broke out in hives and severe itching, but continued using the ointment without any improvement. When seen in the office, I asked him what he was using and he replied, "Vitacilina." He had used Vitacilina ointment years ago for bites and burns and had never had any problems with allergies. He was surprised to learn that about twenty years ago Vitacilina had been reformulated and the original penicillin base substituted with tetracycline. I knew about the formulation change firsthand because of my medical school training in Mexico. Apparently, quite a few people in Mexico had developed allergic reactions to penicillin after having been sensitized to the drug by topical use of Vitacilina. Tetracycline was substituted because of the much lower incidence of tetracycline allergies. Unfortunately, my patient had one. Once he stopped the Vitacilina, the rash disappeared.

On another occasion, while house physician at Lincoln Hospital in the Boyle Heights section of East Los Angeles, I had a patient admitted because of severe headaches, though meningitis had been ruled out. During the taking of the history, the patient mentioned that he had had the headaches for several years, but they now were excruciatingly painful and more frequent, almost daily in the past month, though without any fever. Whenever he saw a physician (usually non-Spanish-speaking), the diagnosis was always the same: migraine. Sometimes treatment brought relief. By now, only narcotic analgesics seemed to work, but they left him so weak and uncoordinated that he could not drive or work. I asked him where he was from, and he mentioned that he was from a small ranch in central Mexico, where his family raised pigs for market. He affirmed that he enjoyed pork and that he would often slaughter the pigs and dress and prepare them for family consumption. This information provided a new avenue for investigation: poorly cooked pork as a source of tapeworm cysts. I immediately ordered a CT scan of the head and a cysticercosis serum titer. Both were positive for cysticercosis. The tapeworm cysts had progressed from his gastrointestinal tract to brain tissue; this was the source of his headaches. Treatment with a new drug called Praziquantel to kill the cysticerci and with corticosteroids to reduce the inflammatory reaction led to a complete resolution of his condition.

Most of my Mexican patients, and some of my first-generation Mexican Americans, will use home remedies with herbs for conditions from colic to diarrhea, coughs, and colds. Chamomile tea is used for colic and upset stomach, as a cleansing agent for eye discharge due to conjunctivitis, or as a sitz bath or poultice for relief of hemorrhoids. Most are surprised at first that I don't scold them for using the home remedies and are most definitely surprised if I actually recommend them as a treatment modality along with more customary medical remedies. I have recommended oregano tea for relief of cough and to help loosen phlegm, and steam baths to loosen phlegm and open nasal passages. I have recommended *té de azahares* for little old ladies who suffer from insomnia and fear addiction to sleeping pills.

I have also found that many of my patients go to Mexican border towns to purchase prescription medicines such as birth control pills, intramuscular injections, antibiotics, blood pressure medications, and others. I find it very handy to keep a current copy of the Mexican *Physicians Desk Reference* (called PLM for short) in my office and refer to it almost daily because of the Latino patient's tendency to self-medicate. Frequently I have to educate the patient, who may have been taking the medication improperly, or may be taking other medications which may cross-react with it. From the patient's perspective, the choice is often an economic one; the patient I place on Zantac 150 twice a day for six to eight weeks at a monthly cost of $80 to $90 may find out that a one-month supply of Zantac in Mexico is $30. And the pharmacies there will usually honor prescriptions from the United States. Thus it may be difficult for the physician to manage his patient effectively, but getting it cheaper in Mexico is a way of life in the border towns and no amount of scolding or education will completely eradicate it. Even non-Latino Americans have caught on to the availability of cheap medicine south of the border and make regular medicine runs to Tijuana or Mexicali.

Another very popular means of lay treatment is the use of *sobadores* or masseuses for treatment of musculoskeletal aches and pains, muscle strains, headaches, and some more esoteric uses like prolapsed uterus or displaced spine. It is very common among Mexicans, but less so among Mexican Americans, to have their aches and pains treated by a sobador who usually gives a ten- to thirty-minute rubdown, kneading and massaging muscle groups in the neck, back, or extremities, in effect relieving muscular spasm and contractures.

The treatments are usually one to three times over a one- or two-week period. Quite often, I see the patients before they receive treatment from the sobadores, who send patients to a physician to rule out fractures, especially if there is severe pain or swelling of a joint or extremity. Once X-rays rule out fractures, dislocations, or scoliosis, I can usually give the patient clearance to have treatment from a sobador. Often, I will suggest a treatment regimen to assist in the healing process, which may involve analgesics or muscle relaxants. Many of my patients are Medi-Cal recipients and as such do not qualify for physical therapy. They find physical therapy too expensive per treatment and prefer a sobador. But even insurance patients may prefer them. Physical therapists only operate during work hours as a rule; patients who must take time off from work to see them often choose a sobador whom they can see after work or on weekends. In addition, insurance patients need not wait up to a month for approval of their physical therapy by an HMO or IPA if they choose a sobador.

I have found over my years of practicing medicine that if you want to be respected by Mexicans, you have to make a sincere effort to learn their language, their customs, their folk medicine, their beliefs, their institutions, their history, and their religion. If you want to be respected by Mexican Americans, you must understand that they have assertive, American-style attitudes acquired through exposure to the media and to the educational system of the United States, and that they have high opinions of what the medical professional can do for them. Sometimes the expectations are unreasonable, but as a society, we believe that anything is possible if we try hard enough. As newcomers to the United States they, too, believe in the dream and are counting on the wonders of American medicine to keep them healthy enough to make it a reality—if God and the Virgin of Guadalupe are willing.

The Meaning of Death

Jerome B. Block

*H*ow many times has the following conversation happened to me at a party:

"Hello! My name is Sam. Who are you?"

"Hello! I am Jerry Block."

"What do you do?"

"Oh, I work at Harbor."

"At what?"

"I am a physician."

"What kind of a physician?"

"I am a good physician."

"No seriously, what do you do?"

"I am a cancer specialist, an oncologist."

"Jeez, you sure have my sympathy! How do you handle all those people dying? I couldn't stand it. Yeeecch."

It's true; a cancer doctor frequently confronts death. But when I first meet a patient, it may also represent a chance at longer life. The physician should not slip too prematurely into the supportive and compassionate role of preparing the patient for death. If death is not in the foreseeable future, it's important to emphasize that fact. I emphasize to my patients that a cure may be possible, that remission leads to increased survival, and that success has been achieved with a variety of cancers. I try to develop behavioral and lifestyle changes in the cancer patient that are likely to contribute to a longer survival and better response to therapy. If the patient can take charge and help forestall death, quality of life is improved by removing the sense of powerlessness that may indeed foster inappropriate hopelessness and early death.

Attitudes like that of my acquaintance Sam about the inevitability of death from a cancer diagnosis are common in all cultures, but if anything this attitude appears to be stronger in Latinos. What are some of the guidelines that seem to work for me in treating Latino cancer patients?

First of all, I try to remember that the physician is often a dominant figure to the patient and family. At the same time, I must resist believing in this intrinsic dominance, as it leads to believing that the patient wants to be like you. Indeed, until you have faced cancer personally, there is no way to predict your own responses. Still, it is unlikely that the physician will share any patient's cultural and socioeconomic responses to cancer, death, and dying. For some, death may be the only rational moment of life, a reward for life or a relief from life, or the ultimate hope of ever understanding life. It is always a surprise to me how few of my patients believe that death is an end to their existence. "There is something else," they say, "to make any sense, there's got to be." At one end of the spectrum, death is a way to join God and the heavenly hosts. At the other, it is simply an "I don't know what will be there." Most, in my experience, believe that there is a "there" there. So I have learned not to question beliefs about what lies ahead but to try to use beliefs to ease passage from life for the patient. I try to say, "You have lived a pure life, kept a good home, loved your children and spouse, respected your God, and been valued by friends." For those patients who believe that cancer and death are a curse, a retribution from God because of error, neglect, or some crime or disrespect, I try to remove their self-judgment from the equation of their passing. If we can discuss this openly, I may be able to relieve a great deal of anxiety through a nonjudgmental interaction.

Understanding the cultural and celebratory aspects of the patient's life have helped me be more effective in dealing with impending death. Certainly the Day of the Dead, celebrated in multiple variations in Latino cultures, is of enormous significance, yet it is largely unknown outside of this culture. I have been to Day of the Dead observations in cemeteries and have seen children playing, people dressed up in their Sunday best, even picnicking at the graveside. Learn what death's role is for your patient and family and help to keep them true to that value. As a doctor, if I can learn what death means to the patient, my own sense of failure, of wanting to flee from the patient's side when the end is coming, is greatly assuaged. Often, patients have comforted me as they lay dying, saying, "I'll be all right; don't worry." This calm acceptance of death has helped me approach the next dying patient.

Pain is always present for the cancer patient approaching death. I try to assure the patient of my skills and the various strategies available for relief from pain. I try to remove any moral stigma or fears of addiction from the use of narcotics, to know my data on pain control and share it with the patient and the family. Pain strips dignity and will; it is what patients fear most. Pain in my patient will mean I have failed; I press the patient to know about his comfort. The patient may not wish to embarrass me by saying, "Your medicine, Doctor, has not made the pain better, even just a little better."

Many of my Latino patients are inseparable from their families. Even if I usually see the patient alone during treatment, I recognize that for many patients, particularly among recent or first- and second-generation Latino immigrants, there is a surprisingly large network of family, friends, and relatives in the background. While often unknown to me, this family is always relevant to the patient's health choices, past, future, and present. At times of death or major illness, this family unit surfaces, often to a surprising degree.

Integration into the American lifestyle can result in dramatic changes for the Latino immigrant, including increased social and economic self-sufficiency. Success for some means standing alone, with limited emotional ties. In my experience, the family of the recently arrived Latino may be surprisingly broad, vital, and fundamental to understanding the patient, and it may differ from that of the U.S.-assimilated patient, who may be relatively more independent. The death of a Latino patient may impact a family in perhaps unanticipated ways; the patient benefits when the physician recognizes the patient's role as a family member. For many of my patients, a part of the entire family dies with them.

One particular incident early in my oncology career brought the importance of the patient's role in the family home to me. I visited the home of one of my patients, who wished to die in the house she'd lived in for more than thirty years. I went for many reasons, but largely because we'd shared a great deal of effort together. When I saw her in my office, she was usually quiet, reserved, thin, and weak from the effects of her disease; she appeared an old woman whose life was flickering away. She usually came to the office alone, and at that time I knew her only from office visits.

When I visited her, she was in her own neatly made bed, with the coverlets carefully folded. The pillows under her head lifted and framed a face that was alert and made luminous by four candles flickering on top of the four corner columns of her bed. The mantel in her room was filled by a shrine, with many other candles lit to honor her saints and objects of religious importance for her. The walls of her room had framed pictures of saints, of her wedding, of her children, of her life as a young girl and woman. She was surrounded by several loving family members, waiting.

In her own home, she was not an old woman whose life was flickering away, but an enthroned queen, preparing, confident and ready, for the next phase of her being—or lack of being. Death seemed to hold no danger, but there was sadness and loss in the family about her bed, at her side. I was struck by the force, the energy, and the affirmation of a life that I sensed in that room. Clearly, while valued and appreciated, my visit was not a comfort to the patient or the family; they needed no comfort from me now. She needed none of my skills and gave me a gift by showing me who she was now and would forever be in her family's eyes.

I have found that the Latino family appreciates truth. Truth permits the family to know that they did all that could have been done or all that the patient wanted. Truth is important, even in those situations in which the family asks you not to tell the patient about chances for survival, care, or your own prognosis. The modern U.S.-trained physician may come into the profession believing that the primary responsibility is to the patient, but one quickly learns that there are sensitive situations where the Latino patient's own primary interests are those of the family, not of self. The wise physician should not separate a patient's care from the effects of such actions on the family. To do so would fail both the patient and the family.

I always respect the intelligence of the patient and the surrounding family or extended support group. If a physician is not fluent in Spanish, interactions with Latinos may be in English. If either the patient or family is not comfortable in English, they may have trouble asking questions or requesting information, and may need amplification of the physician's remarks or plans. Indeed, some Latino patients and families may exhibit what is clearly an uncharacteristic reserve or passivity when faced with a non-Latino physician whose decisions have (often) life-and-death import for themselves or their loved ones. I have observed physicians oversimplify, or become excessively paternalistic in discussions or explanations, thinking that limited verbal communication reflects a limited intelligence or educational level. The more one can approach the Latino cancer patient as an equal partner in care, the more likely it is that treatment will be successful, whatever exigencies accrue.

Patients want a relationship with their doctor; they want them to take time, to care, to be involved with them. The Latino patient, particularly, does not want a physician to be simply a dispenser of data, opinions, risks, medicines, and bills. However, relationships require investment of "emotional coin" by the physician, and for cancer doctors that investment in the patient is usually met in the end by death. Those physicians who believe their goal is to prolong life almost always fail. They find that the more they have invested of themselves in the patient relationship, the more destructive it is to the physician on the death of that patient. Oncologists learn noninvolvement and may seem nonemotional, noncaring, nonloving in their delivery of medical care, when in fact they are simply erecting a self-preservation mechanism. So the emotional exchange that may be vital to the patient's quality of life is hard to get from the experienced oncologist. Other doctors, nurses, even receptionists may offer the emotional strength the patient needs and looks for; aware oncologists will see that this support is provided if they cannot do it themselves.

There comes a time in the care of cancer when both the patient and the physician know that death is on its inexorable way. The doctor's medicines have failed, any relationship that has evolved between doctor and patient is about to be severed, the doctor wants to flee the examination room and the joking, the sharing, the touching. How many oncologists have had to fight this urge to withdraw when their patients "fail to do well"? How does this retreat by the physician fit into the dying process? Is it good, bad, or necessary? The patient may sense a change in the physician's attitude and if so, the physician must, even wrenchingly, address this behavior and change it to meet the patient's needs and concerns. If the dying patient is conscious—or if family are in the room—I always spend time, examine the patient, and make comments that are hopefully not too full of platitudes. Death mandates a new wavelength, one different from the shared interaction during the positive treatment phases of active care. The challenge of a patient's dying is indeed a greater one for the physician than the challenge of providing quality, active anticancer therapy.

The care of the Latino patient with cancer, especially the patient who is preparing to die with cancer, is more successful if the physician can demonstrate caring, respect, and acknowledgment of the patient's separateness. By addressing and examining our own beliefs, physicians can avoid error and deliver those key aspects of psychosocial and physiologic therapy that serve the patient best. Finally, consider your patients as much as possible as equals who can help make important statements on the adequacy of therapy and outcome, whatever the clinical situation.

* * *

Dr. Jerome Block died unexpectedly on January 29, 2005, at age seventy-two. He left behind his loving wife of forty-six years, Arlene, as well as a son, two daughters, three adoring grandchildren, and two sisters. He was a member of Temple Beth El in San Pedro, California. His family remembers him for his love and commitment to them as well as his innumerable interests, inimitable sense of humor, and tremendous kindness.

Cada Cabeza Es un Mundo
Everyone Lives a Different Reality

Irene Redondo-Churchward

Mira como ando mujer, por tu querer

borracho y apasionado no mas por tu amor

Mira como ando mi bien, perdido a la borrachera y a la perdición.

So begins an old Mexican favorite, "Tú, Solo Tú." Loosely translated, the song tells of a man who has become a drunk, a lost soul, because the woman doesn't love him—and it is her fault.

I remember singing that song as a duet with my father at family gatherings when I was young. I never thought much about the words then. Just recently, however, I heard a girl of eleven singing this same song on television with a mariachi band. But now, it simultaneously saddened and angered me that in spite of so many efforts, so many of us fail to see how inappropriate it is for a young child to be singing this song.

How can so many fail to see the connection between our cultural traditions, expressed in some of our songs, and the perpetuation of one of the most serious problems facing Latinos today—alcohol abuse?

I am a Mexican American woman born in Tucson, Arizona, sixty miles from the border town of Nogales, Sonora. Even as a child, I was aware that alcohol was a major part of every significant event in *la familia*. At every occasion, from weddings to baptisms, from birthdays to funerals, liquor was always present. For the most part, it didn't present a problem, unless it was abused. The Spanish-language movies and the music of that time further reinforced the cultural acceptability of using alcohol to cope with the stresses in life—as well as for all celebrations— which was consistent with the reality I saw growing up. We sang songs like "Andale," which glorified *borracheras*, or drunken episodes. (Linda Ronstadt's 1990s big seller, "Canciones de mi Padre," included this old favorite as well as "Tú, Solo Tú").

Then there were *dichos*, or sayings, passed along by our mothers and grandmothers, which instilled values and taught children the difference between acceptable and unacceptable behavior. Dichos are a tremendous Latino cultural strength that can mold behavior without lecturing or confrontation. *Cada cabeza es un mundo* (Each mind is a world unto itself) helped me learn to value the uniqueness of every individual, advice that has served me well in my career. But like many other aspects of Latino culture, *dichos* serve as yet another reinforcement of prevailing cultural attitudes toward alcohol: *Para boca de borracho, oídos de cantinero* (Listen to a drunk as a bartender would, without taking his insults too seriously), or *El panadero se emborracha de gusto cuando sale bueno el pan, y de pesar cuando sale malo* (The baker gets drunk for joy when the bread is well baked, and for sorrow when it isn't baked well).

It was also in my youth that I learned it was inappropriate for my mother, grandmothers, aunts—or any woman, for that matter—to indulge in alcohol use. In my family, alcohol was strictly reserved for males. On the rare occasion when a woman did drink, and maybe drank a little too much, the double standard was clear. Alcohol use by women was not tolerated in the way its use was by men, who were excused for inappropriate or offensive behavior while under the influence of liquor.

There was also a big difference between the occasional binge drinking, resulting in drunkenness, that takes place at social events and the drinking of a *borracho*—a drunk. In those years, I never heard the word *alcoholico*, or alcoholic.

Because of a bicultural upbringing, I also observed quite readily that the Latino prohibition on female drinking was at odds with dominant American culture. An avid moviegoer, I could see in English-language movies that women drank easily at social events, and I often thought it strange that their behavior was not seen as an aberration. However, these women suffered the same intolerance and lack of respect as Latinas if they became inebriated. Again, men's alcoholic capers were often overlooked, considered humorous or dismissed, while women's were viewed with great contempt.

My growing awareness of alcohol abuse and the problems it causes started when I realized that in spite of the fun and laughter of most family occasions, they also seemed to ignite a combative spirit in some of my family members and friends, who became argumentative when they had had too much to drink. They became *necios* or *pesados* (overbearing). In addition, when a very good high school friend of mine was killed in a car accident caused by drinking and driving, I was devastated by the senselessness of his death. But, at that point, I could not imagine myself trying to combat alcohol and alcohol-related problems. It was too much a part of the culture.

One important and consistent element in any study of Latino culture, especially that of Mexican Americans, is the role of family. So much revolves around the strengths of the family; it is central to making progress with an alcoholic's recovery issues. It is also important to understand that the more traditional the family, the more hierarchical it is, the higher the status of the men within it will be. This, I believe, has led many to make incorrect assumptions about the Latino man, and has resulted in the term *macho* being defined in negative terms: physically aggressive, domineering, arrogant, a womanizer. It is rarely, if ever, used as a positive description of anyone.

Yet many of us learned growing up that *macho* was synonymous with being a "real man." It defined a responsible man of dignity and a loving, protective father. Such a man also had a strong work ethic and was a good provider who lived up to his responsibilities (*cumplía con su deber*). In addition, he was respectful of others and a man of his word. However, *macho* could also be used to describe a man who could drink excessively without negative effects. In other words, a man who possessed the positive *macho* qualities could also drink heavily and this would be not only acceptable but further proof of his manhood. This image is reinforced by the media and in marketing efforts that target the Latino population.

Such inconsistencies in the perception of alcohol and alcohol use can make it difficult to address alcohol issues in a traditional Latino *familia*. Since the overall cultural perception of an alcoholic is someone who is weak, who has lost control and dignity, those with an alcohol problem are not likely to seek help. However, due to drinking and driving and similar problems, many are court mandated to enroll in alcohol recovvery programs. Once enrolled in a program that understands the cultural context in which their heavy drinking occurs, these individuals can begin the educational process that leads to recovery.

Juan could never reconcile his drinking problem with his view of his responsibilities as a man. In his estimation, it was a moral issue, because he never missed work and didn't mistreat his family. Heavy alcohol use could not possibly "be a problem." All the men in his family were heavy drinkers, he indicated, and it was never seen as a problem for them. Drinking was the acceptable way of releasing the stress of working hard all week.

Juan spoke of growing up in a rural area of Mexico where it was a source of pride when a man could take his young son with him to drink at a local cantina. This was a man's way of showing off his male offspring to others. As a father who loved his son very much, Juan would thus model drinking for his son, as his own father had done with him. The ritual seemed desirable to Juan, part of the rites of passage to manhood. Yes, it was true some men were not as good at holding their liquor as others, but he definitely felt he was not in that category and neither would any of his five sons ever be, since he had taught them well.

Juan dismissed arguments at home about his drinking as his wife trying to control him and that, of course, wasn't going to work. He not only saw nothing wrong with his drinking, he strongly defended the practice. Yet, further exploration with Juan revealed the severe toll alcohol was taking on his health. When he was diagnosed by his physician with cirrhosis of the liver, Juan still denied the damage could have been alcohol related. For him, alcohol-related problems were what *borrachos*, irresponsible men who did not take care of their families, experienced.

Ultimately, encouraging Juan to contextualize the problem as one of his body being allergic to alcohol helped him maintain his dignity and set him on the road to recovery. Having a bilingual/bicultural alcohol-recovery specialist helped considerably in this case.

Alberto had been in this country for five years when he received a drunk-driving citation that brought him to our program. He talked about how heavy a drinker he had been in his hometown in Zacatecas. But when he started to experience blackouts, he became worried and went to see his priest. He spoke about the written *juramento* (vow) he made to God. The process involved him taking a friend with him as a sponsor who witnessed the written vow, which he carried with him at all times. When his friends invited him to go out and drink, his *juramento* gave him the power to refuse. His friends respected his decision. They would leave him alone and not exert pressure, as they saw this as a sacred vow to God that should not be interfered with.

Alberto eventually came to the United States to find a better life for himself, though he had to leave his family behind. He made many adjustments to the culture, but under the stress of working up to seven days a week at times and living without his family, he began drinking again. He did not feel that this drinking was out of control, but had recently noticed he could not remember what he had done the night before. This caused him a great deal of concern.

If he were back in his hometown, Alberto said, he would go back to the priest and renew his *juramento*. But he didn't feel the same comfort with the church here. In Zacatecas, the church was the focal point of family traditions and the centerpiece of all community events. Here, he did not feel a part of what went on in the church. Eventually he discovered a fundamentalist Christian group for recovering individuals. Here he found the communal spirit and the support he was looking for, and it assisted him greatly in his recovery.

Latinos overall seem to be on both ends of the continuum of drinking patterns. They are either abstainers or heavy drinkers, but women account for the greater portion of the former, due in great measure to the cultural sanctions against alcohol use among women. However, the more acculturated the Latina becomes, the more likely she is to develop alcohol-related problems.

Carmen, a second-generation Mexican American business professional who became part of our task force, shared how she became an alcoholic when she started to climb the corporate ladder. She found herself pressured to drink at numerous meetings, both during lunch and after work. Then there were the many business events she was expected to attend. She found herself complying with increased frequency to the pressure to drink. She felt the need to keep up with what she described as "the boys." The need to prove that she, as a woman and as a Latina, could hang in there with the best of them caused her tremendous problems.

Carmen would return from a two-martini lunch to find her business judgment already affected. After work, she would have a few drinks to wind down. She was strong; she could handle it with "the best of them." However, the shame of becoming an alcoholic was starting to eat at her, compounded by her family's intolerance of drinking for women in general and for Carmen in particular. On a downward spiral in her career and her personal life, she felt isolated and alone. In her desperation, she felt she had no one to turn to for help. She made the decision to stop drinking by herself, cold turkey. But without a support system to turn to, she was having trouble staying sober.

Coincidentally, she heard about a conference planned by a group of Latinas who were trying to help educate others with alcohol-related problems. Thus Carmen became part of our planning committee and began to share her experiences with others in similar circumstances. She shared her story at the conference and learned that most of the participants had been taught the same contradictory values when it came to women drinking. She helped other Latinas see how they could turn to each other during the recovery process, since they were unable to turn to their own families. Carmen's involvement in our program steadied her and made her progress possible.

Finally, Maria came to us seeking help. She had found half-empty liquor bottles in unusual places, evidence that her mother was drinking secretly. Yet how could she talk to her mother about what she saw? It was highly unacceptable to bring her mother's behavior into question. Furthermore, since "women weren't supposed to drink," it was better for all concerned to pretend it wasn't happening. Even when it became apparent that the mother, Rosa, was showing the effects of heavy drinking, and other members of the family were also noticing it, no one was able to confront her. They mostly worried she might fall or hurt herself in some other way. The family fiercely protected the sacredness of the mother, but ironically, their protection enabled the drinking to continue.

Though she knew her mother needed help, the concept of enabling was very difficult for Maria to grasp. How could it possibly be wrong to provide supportive actions to a family member who was in trouble? Isn't that what families do? She and her brothers and sisters had been taught to help each other, regardless of the situation. The idea that the family's inability to confront their mother was exacerbating her drinking problem was inconceivable. Confrontation would be humiliating; who would want to humiliate their mother? Codependency, as a concept, was diametrically opposed to everything Maria had been taught. A woman's role is to help the family function. Since it protected her mother from humiliation, how could her silence possibly be viewed as detrimental?

Eventually we were able to get Maria and Rosa to attend a mother and daughter conference focusing on alcohol-related problems by explaining that it would be an educational opportunity they could share with each other. We felt this would be a less confrontational beginning. After all, confrontation works only with those who value it as a means of resolving problems. Others need a gentler, less threatening approach that doesn't destroy the dignity of the individual.

Rosa later shared with me that she finally learned the magnitude of the destruction one person's drinking can cause for family members. She also learned that she was not alone. She related most especially to a conference participant who described her own downward spiral with alcohol, which she felt came from trying to cope with alienation and discrimination, and from frustration at her failure to negotiate the systems in this country. Her daughter Maria learned to integrate her positive family values with her image of herself as a woman, all the while developing the healthy outlook that will permit her to resist enabling behaviors.

Tamales for Health

America Bracho

I went first so that everyone could understand the exercise.

"Hello. My name is America. I am from Venezuela. My favorite food is *arepas*, my favorite hobby is dancing, and I am the director of Latino Health Access."

Then each one of the students shared their names, where they were from, their favorite food, their favorite hobby. Finally, seated in a circle, the participants told us what diabetes meant for them. When his turn arrived, the old gentleman seated to my right said, "What is diabetes for me? Aaaay—I remember my mother in a wheelchair, blind because of the insulin. They gave her first this thing, then something else, but nothing worked." Then it was the turn of the tall woman from Michoacán, who loved *tacos dorados* with *salsa fresca* and whose favorite hobby was to knit: "I am very nervous. I make little balls of string to calm my nerves. I think that I have had this illness because I am so nervous. My aunt also got diabetes when they told her that her daughter had been run over while she was traveling to Saguayo."

A woman from Guadalajara, who loved to dance and who was frightened by the idea of dying and leaving three young daughters, shared her story. A man spoke who had discovered he had diabetes only when he was hospitalized after having lost consciousness. Next came a man who said that he had been cured of diabetes by taking the herbal remedy *uña de gato* and drinking *agua de nopales* (cactus juice), but he had become ill once again from diabetes because his son had become a gang member.

The stories continued. As part of our educational strategy for the control of diabetes, the sessions last for two hours, once a week, for twelve weeks. Participants are sent to us from various community clinics, churches, and neighborhood organizations. Our classes, begun in 1994, are always full in spite of the fact that the majority of Latino diabetics do not know that they have this condition. Here in Orange County, where the American Diabetes Association estimates that there are over 70,000 Latinos with diabetes, Latino Health Access offers the only full-scale program designed to educate Latinos affected by a disease that, when uncontrolled, can result in blindness, limb amputation, renal problems, and finally death.

Diabetes is a chronic disease. There is no cure for it. Control of diabetes depends primarily on the lifestyle of the patient, which means the patient, his family, and his community must be involved. Yet we live in a society where health services are designed to provide rapid solutions to specific, isolated problems. We'd like to fix everything with a shot. We wish there were a shot for diabetes, an immunization against alcoholism, a shot for children who don't listen to us, a shot against poverty. But these immunizations don't exist. Even if solutions could be found in medication, social context would still be crucial, as access to medication, understanding, and compliance must come from the patient. Solutions must deal with the complex systems in which we live. They must be holistic.

When a patient has diabetes (or any other chronic disease), the path ahead does not include a cure, but rather a lifelong process of maintaining health in the face of disease. The patient's social context—knowledge, social support, financial and psychological resources, perceptions of reality—affects the outcome. Often, we must change the patient's image of illness, of family dynamics, and even of the role of providers to initiate involvement. We must show the diabetic that managing illness is now part of his life, and therefore part of the life of his family and his community. As health providers, we should welcome the contextualization of this illness, for if the patient understands the importance of his social nexus in his care, the solution will be contextualized too.

But why is it so hard to work holistically? For one thing, it goes against the grain of our training as health professionals, which has encouraged us to divide everything, including the human body, into compartments. And while it is true that a heart surgeon should concentrate on the heart, it is also true that a disequilibrium in the rest of the body and its fluids can kill the patient even though the heart operation might have technically been a "success."

Our training—and our society—has also encouraged us to see physicians as gods; after all, they do cure disease. The ability to cure a patient is gratifying for all providers, as it satisfies our need for acknowledgment, power, and success. Of course, if we were to redefine the curing of a patient as a process in which a physician has only one part, control and power would have to be shared with the patient. And if we were to go even further and speak of health, in a holistic sense, as physical, mental, and social well-being rather than the mere absence of disease, then health would be de-medicalized even more.

To the extent that we, as medical professionals, incorporate the patient, his family, and his community in solving health

problems, we are most effective, especially with chronic conditions like diabetes. In order to achieve this mobilization of
patient, family, and community, health practitioners have to
be more socially oriented, more humane, more humble, and
even more self-critical. We have to listen more. And we have
to listen to more than just words. We have to facilitate and
motivate the behavior of others. We have to look beyond our
own actions as providers.

But just as we begin to discuss a more holistic definition
of health, we begin to hear physicians complaining that they
don't have time for more areas of concern. Social context is
not their job; they are not social workers. Yet those providers
who do invest their time in understanding the world from the
perspective of the patient obtain much more satisfactory results.
Solutions begin to suggest themselves. When the gentleman
from Zacatecas who loves baseball says diabetes robs him of
the desire to work, then the treatment plan necessarily ought to
include the desire to work as an indicator of improvement. This
is the indicator that the patient wants. The clinical indicator, a
desired level of hemoglobin A, cannot be the sole indicator of
the quality of life.

Instead of looking at our community from a deficit perspective, Latino Health Access sees each one of the participants,
their values and strengths, as the pillars of a treatment and
maintenance plan. An intervention is only as useful as the
degree to which we appreciate and utilize the skills, experiences, and perspectives of patients to help solve their own
problems. During sessions, we identify the strengths of every
single participant. For some, these might include their desire
to live, to learn, or to work, or their love of family. Others'
strengths might come from actions: crossing the border without
papers to search for a better future, participating in class, trying
new recipes, or complying with an exercise plan.

Our diabetes program, based on the principles of adult education, begins quietly but gradually teaches participants to give their opinions with complete frankness. Dignity, respect, caring, and good relationships are hallmarks of our program. It's a family environment where we know each other's names, where there are kisses and hugs when people enter. Questions such as "How do people exercise?" don't threaten us, aren't ridiculed, and are answered by all. Participants share a profound conviction that we all have an important role to play in the control of this disease. Our participants know that they are in our classes so that they can die *with* diabetes, not *because* of diabetes.

I remember as if it were yesterday the señora from Sonora whose favorite food was pork *pozole* and whose hobby was being with her grandchildren. This señora was very, very quiet and wouldn't participate. We tried various strategies to draw her into the class, but none of them gave any results. One day, it occurred to us to ask the class if they knew the song "México Lindo y Querido." Everyone in the class said yes. One of our participants began, "Voz de la guitarra, mia, al despertar la mañana." The woman from Sonora stood up from her chair, closed her eyes, and began to sing with all her might: "Vengo a cantar la alegría de mi tierra mexicana." As she continued singing, the other students were astounded by the emotion this quiet woman showed as she sang. When she reached the ending, "México lindo y querido, si muero lejos de tí/que digan que estoy dormida y que me devuelvan a tí," the señora sat down, and she cried as I have rarely seen. She began to tell us of her loneliness in this country, how much she missed the children and grand-children on the other side, in Mexico. As she opened up and voiced her unhappiness, her participation in the class began. Of course, the impact of our program and her capacity to control her diabetes improved.

One day, we were teaching the use of the glucose meter (all patients receive a glucometer either free or at very low cost thanks to program funds or an arrangement with a clinic). The señora from Veracruz was allowing her daughter, who accompanied her to class, to do the exam. I let it pass. At the next class, the daughter did not come, and the señora did not wish to do the exam. She was a little angry with her daughter, she explained, because she hadn't come to class, and in fact, she had to plead with her daughter to help her with the exam at home. Why? The señora from Veracruz did not know how to read numbers.

We explained to her how to write the numbers and even sent homework to her house. To be honest, the señora wasn't very happy, but she did what we asked. She brought the homework to the next class, and we began to teach her to use the glucose meter. She was able to write down on the paper a numeral two, a numeral one, a numeral zero—just what the glucometer had read. Her new skill would now make the monitoring possible. The señora beamed with happiness, and I think it was the happiness of becoming a little bit more independent.

The señora from Durango said that she couldn't come to the classes because she had to take care of her grandchildren. Because her adult daughter earned money for the family, the least she could do was take care of the house and the grandchildren. This is an attitude we frequently see in our Latinas: first comes the family, second comes the family, and after that comes the family. Therefore, in our program, family is a key concept. We don't tell Latinas that they should think of themselves first. Instead, we tell them that it's absolutely the best thing to love their families, but the greatest proof of that love is to take care of themselves. That way, they can take better care of their loved ones. When we cook with less grease, when we eat more vegetables, we are not a burden on our families. On the contrary, we are investing in the health of the ones that we love, who also happen to be the families of diabetics.

In class, we tell students that if they can learn words in English such as "green card" or "social security," they can also learn expressions such as "protein in the urine." If they can't remember the phrase, that's okay, but they must ask again and again, and eventually they will learn it. The patients laugh and learn. But they begin to negotiate for themselves in the exam room with the physician. And in so doing, they announce their right to become part of the team in the management of their own diabetes.

Insulin management by diabetics is one of the areas in which lack of compliance by the patient is extremely frustrating for the providers. Our program has been successful in changing that dynamic. But this is where we begin: "Insulin makes people blind." "They gave insulin to my aunt and a month later she began to lose her vision." "You become an addict once you begin using it." "It causes people to lose their respect for you when they see you injecting. They see you as very, very weak." "I have a friend who used insulin at work, and everyone talks bad about him."

For almost two hours, students work to understand what insulin is, how it is used, and what it is good for. They learn that everyone has insulin in the body and to distinguish insulin from drugs, substances that the body does not need. We need insulin, but if the body is not producing it, we must provide it. Finally, they understand that the aunt became blind not because of insulin, but because her uncontrolled diabetes damaged her eyes. They learned that instead of blaming insulin, they should blame the glucose or sugar in the blood for the damage it causes. Some of our health promoters also reveal that they suffered damage to their own eyes because they had never received insulin. At the end of the session the participants are more open to insulin use, even though it is not preferred.

Their physicians report a better acceptance of insulin; in fact, in some cases a request for insulin came from patients who finally understood the dangers of high sugar levels and decided it was better to take insulin than go blind.

A while back, a doctor called me from one of the clinics that sends patients to us and told me how pleased and impressed he was with our program. He was delighted to see normal sugar values, and improvement in hemoglobin A1C, in his patients. Patients told him what they had learned and how they were incorporating changes into their lives as a result of the classes. The doctor also acknowledged how frustrated he was that he had encouraged the same changes for years without results. Three months later, this doctor had changed practices, and he called me again to tell me how much he missed his active, informed, and capable patients. He said, "I was just beginning to enjoy conversations with informed patients, having the luxury of making plans with the patient in monitoring their progress. Now I feel like I have gone backwards. Now I have to deal with patients who don't know where they are. America, when is Latino Health Access going to give classes in this part of town?"

My role in the program is that of a public health educator. As a young adult in Venezuela, I chose to study medicine because I wished to help people regain their health, and medical school helped me further define my role. I graduated knowing that I didn't want to be a goddess or saint, and with the conviction that healing goes beyond mere medicines and techniques. I wanted to help people make decisions and create their own road to a more healthful life. I wanted to help people to help themselves, their families, and communities to be healthier. My work as a physician in Venezuela helped me realize that educating consumers about health issues is the best way of advocating for improved access and quality in the health care system. I came to the United States to do a master's program in public health at the University of Michigan, convinced that I wanted to educate in health at the community level. Since then, I have devoted my work exclusively to public health.

After directing programs in AIDS control in Detroit for over four years, I became even more determined to become a defender of the rights of patients and their families. The AIDS epidemic has demonstrated that when patients are informed they can change their lives, their behavior, even FDA regulations. Patients struggling for their health and for their lives can even influence Congress. I learned that one infected person is the best teacher for another infected person. I learned that patients can learn about T4 cells, protease inhibitors, and Kaposi's sarcoma. With admiration, I remember how people living with HIV took over scientific AIDS conferences and openly protested the lack of inclusion of infected persons (PWA, Persons with AIDS). It was the people with AIDS who finally forced the professional community to discuss not only the clinical but also the human face of AIDS. Everyone's consciousness grew. Now, every new death or infection due to AIDS is converted into the face of the child, the lover, the father, the mother of someone. The AIDS epidemic also has taught us that our communities have consistently been ignored and that unless we take leadership, resources will never flow to them. Those who are most affected have to offer leadership.

Diabetes is not very different. We are speaking of a chronic disease over which the medical and pharmaceutical communities have a tremendous power, a disease in which the life of the señor from San Salvador who liked *pupusas*, became blind and alcoholic, and died, leaving two small children without support, is not important. None of this is a problem of science and is not discussed at conferences about diabetes. Congress provides a laughably small amount of funding for diabetes;

the CDC passively assigns and distributes these monies to the states. This small budget provides only weak strategies that have little impact on one of the most devastating diseases in the Latino community.

The AIDS epidemic has shown that changes in national policy will only come when those most affected take action. That's why our program emphasizes patient control and the skills to negotiate with physicians and providers. In fact, we make an effort to identify and encourage participants who have leadership qualities. It's quite easy to recognize them. By the second class, they are the participants who offer to help. Those who know how to read offer to help those who do not; those who are a little bit more calm are able to console those who cry; those who quickly understand the use of the glucometer help others who seem to be having some difficulty. By the third class, they may offer to arrange the tables or perhaps bring some food for snacks. The participants with obvious leadership skills begin to give their opinions, to question themselves, the clinics, their families. These future leaders want to do something now, both for themselves and for the others. We offer them this opportunity through further training.

Once recruited and trained as "health promoters" or "community health workers" using the WHO model, these leaders—we call them *promotoras*—help give classes and do follow-up with participants. We feel that the use of *promotoras* has contributed to the success of our program. In fact, in 1998 the American Diabetes Association recognized the *promotoras* with the Community Empowerment Award for their effective work in the fight against diabetes. Nine of them have been hired by Latino Health Access.

Many physicians and other providers have difficulty accepting the fundamental importance of patient empowerment in our program. One example of it is the team plan form. This is a

triplicate form used to record clinical information, lab information, and any other general recommendations in the patient's
file. One copy goes to the patient, who has been taught to
understand the contents. The initial provider response to the
team plan form is a fear that the patients are going to read material that is in their patient file. After that comes a questioning
of the ability of patients to understand technical information.
But when they accept the team plan form, providers delight
in their successful interventions with informed patients. Use of
this form has helped, bit by bit, to raise the quality of services
for patients.

One day, I received a call informing me that one of our
students had suddenly gone blind. Her daughter informed me
that she no longer went to classes but needed help. I asked the
woman, who had been a diabetic for the last ten years, if she
had known of the problem with her eyes. She told me she had
never been examined. In talking with her health care provider,
I discovered that diabetics weren't receiving eye examinations
annually because the clinic simply didn't believe the patients
could manage the treatment of these sorts of complications. I
felt frustrated. This condescending attitude correlated with so
many others I had witnessed in which patients have not been
informed of their problems because it was assumed that they
were incapable of being part of the solution. And when the
patients are low-income Latinos, the attitudes are even worse.
I sat down right then and wrote out the educational module
for patients about their eyes and feet.

As part of the eye awareness program, we informed participants that if, for example, they were diagnosed with retinopathy
and required laser surgery, the cost could be $4,000. We asked
what they would do if they were told they needed such an
expensive treatment. The gentleman from Tamaulipas who
loved boxing told us that he would return to Mexico to have

the treatment in the Social Security hospital. The woman from
Guerrero said that she would sell her furniture and go into debt.
But the reply from the señor from Chihuahua impacted not
only the class but also the direction of Latino Health Access.
This gentleman said, "I would have this surgery even if I had
to sell tamales." In his response, he reflected a philosophy of
life in the Latino community: when something needs to be
done, we don't stand around with our arms crossed. To say
that he would have the operation even if he had to sell tamales
expressed the determination, the responsibility, the capacity
to resolve problems, and the humility and the pride that is
ours. One month after this experience, Latino Health Access
launched its first fund-raising campaign, called Tamales for
Health. The campaign has been carried on for a number of
years and has managed to capture the attention of the media
and influential people in the community. During our annual
kick off, we have had the director of the Orange County Public
Health Department, members of the board of supervisors, local
leaders, and celebrities elbow to elbow with our people. The
campaign has allowed us to help patients with laser surgery for
their eyes; hundreds have received their annual podiatric and
dental examinations with money raised from our Aunque Tenga
Que Vender Tamales campaign.

In 1997, the diabetes self-management program received
the Society of Public Health Education Award as the National
Program of Excellence. LHA has several programs in addition
to those related to chronic diseases. The strategy to achieve a
healthier community includes the first Healthy Community
project in Orange County as a partnership with the Public
Health Department. The project intends to intervene compre-
hensively at the community level, addressing issues of education,
recreation, health, safety, and more in one of the poorest neighborhoods of this county, the 92701 zip code in Santa Ana.

Again, our program benefits individuals and families and is based on the assets they bring to the table.

We have found that the main supporters of the Healthy Community project are our former diabetes students. They are helping to mobilize the community. By recognizing people's strengths and facilitating their involvement in the resolution of their problems, hope for a better future is established. If people have hope, they will continue moving ahead without us and we can move on to help other communities. We are committed to fostering independence, community control, solidarity, and self-reliance. Together with our community, Latino Health Access continues to work toward a healthier world—even if we have to sell tamales.

We Talked About Our Lives, Our Dreams, Our Disappointments

Mercedes Brenneisen-Goode

When I attended medical school in Peru, my education did not include instructions on how to deal with the emotional needs of patients. Rather, my training emphasized how to diagnose and how to cure illness. After I started to practice, I found out that one could always refer patients to social workers or to clergy to deal with "emotional" issues. Because of the medical hierarchy, doctors were almost encouraged to avoid dealing with incurable disease and death issues. Over the past twenty years, I have come to realize that for my Latino patients, it is precisely the ability to deal with these issues that distinguishes a really effective physician.

Patients dealing with incurable disease and cancer, no matter what their race, want to hear words of hope and encouragement. For the most part, they are not interested in the latest statistics about survival or disease response to particular drugs. They want doctors to see them as unique individuals with rich lives, now confronting what may be the final chapter of those lives. When told they have cancer, all patients react in a similar fashion. To varying degrees, they all express disbelief in their diagnosis. A period of denial ensues. This is followed by a need to lay blame somewhere for this terrible illness. Anxiety and anger are part of this phase. Many individuals go on to experience profound feelings of depression, despair, and hopelessness, and it is often in this state of mind that they are introduced to the concepts of treatment. Most patients eventually come to accept their illness. With this acceptance comes a desire to fight back and triumph over illness. At this point, the patient wants specific guidance on how to win this battle.

Each patient has different coping mechanisms, but common to most Latino patients is a strong religious faith and a belief in nontraditional medical therapies. These coping measures are often firmly in place before the patient comes to my office. Often, they have consulted an herbalist, a chiropractor, and a local pharmacist. They may have started some form of herbal treatment on the advice of family or friends. I encourage those with religious faith to let God help them. I exhort them to put aside their desire to control everything and to focus attention on their family relationships and their spiritual beliefs. For the nonbeliever, death tends to be much harder to accept. But whatever the patient's religious conviction or background may be, each person brings a range of experiences and viewpoints to the doctor's office.

Latino patients, like any other patient group, may not possess a great deal of medical sophistication or knowledge of disease.

However, my Latino patients often have their own ideas about cancer and how it is treated. They may have seen someone close to them who has suffered with this dreadful disease or may know someone who was "cured" of it. In the latter case, the curative treatment, no matter how improbable, will influence how they want their own illnesses treated. It is precisely this lack of sophistication that compels them to trust their doctors for their knowledge, guidance, and reassurance.

Latino patients put their lives in the hands of their physicians, and do not question the decisions that are made. They do not necessarily seek out the latest therapies in the medical literature, and are not comfortable with a practitioner who spouts data about the latest drug or treatment modality. Rather, they want a physician who is warm and affectionate, who explains things so that they can be understood. The most common complaint that I hear from my Latino patients is that they do not understand their diagnosis or, even worse, that they have never been informed. Sometimes this can be attributed to the informing physician's language skills. Perhaps denial is responsible. But more often than not, the physicians have not taken the time to explain things clearly. Yet even if the physician has explained the diagnosis fully and the patient understands it, there is likely to be much more acceptance if the patient is given reason to hope, reason to believe that their suffering can be controlled.

Many patients have been referred to me by family doctors in whom they have complete trust. That trust is in turn passed on to me. Along with this conferred trust comes a level of expectation that I will render the same type of service as the family physician. While the family physician may not be a state-of-the-art practitioner, he or she is looked upon as a well-known and well-loved member of the family. Often, a hug and a kiss are exchanged when arriving at the office, a physical demonstration that the patient has put his or her well-being in the hands of the trusted physician. This degree of familiarity and trust is not as common among non-Latinos or even second-generation Latinos.

The initial interview with the patient must include information on belief systems, coping mechanisms, and approaches to therapy. Only through this exchange can the patient and the physician find common ground and establish guidelines for treatment. It's important for the physician to allow the patient to hope. Hope empowers the patient. Hope also gives the patients permission to incorporate their religious beliefs into an entire treatment plan, which often results in a more positive outcome. I strongly encourage my patients to rely on spiritual guidance for healing and coping.

I try to encourage my patients and their families to participate actively in their care. I tell them to do nice things for themselves, to pray, to eat well, and to exercise. I do not discourage the use of herbs or other less conventional medical therapeutics unless I perceive them to be counterproductive. I let them know that their lives are in God's hands and that doctors are merely his instruments, trained specifically to help care for the ill. I let them know that doctors do not predict the future, and I do not make pronouncements about how long I think one has to live, although I am willing to discuss the statistical expectations. Most of all, I encourage my patients with stories about patients I have seen in my medical practice, many of whom have found great benefit in the combination of alternative approaches to their diseases.

How much can hope do in the treatment of cancer? I can provide many examples. One is Ruben, thirty-seven, an Argentinean who has been battling malignant meningioma for the past nine years. He has undergone eight craniotomies, a full course of radiation therapy to his brain, and gamma knife radiosurgery. He is now free of tumor, but he is paralyzed in all his extremities except for his right hand. He has been on chronic steroids for treatment-related radiation necrosis and has gained an enormous amount of weight. He is extremely weak, grossly Cushingoid, and has many reasons to be depressed, but through all of his trials, he has maintained a positive attitude. He spends his whole day on the computer, investigating medical therapies and equipment that might help him with his condition, and he communicates to others in similar circumstances. Through the Internet, he has found a device that enables his very tiny wife to lift him from his bed to his wheelchair so he can get around on his own.

Ruben is always telling jokes and laughs a lot. He told me that his sense of humor has seen him through some very dark days. Ruben and his family know that he will very likely die either from brain edema or from opportunistic infections, but he lives each day of his life as a contented husband, father, and cancer survivor. He still asks me to participate in all of his treatment decisions and trusts me implicitly. He has even introduced me to the Internet and serves as my problem solver over the telephone. I have told him on several occasions that I need just a little piece of his brain to become more computer literate. He replies that he has already given his share. We now correspond with each other on the Internet quite regularly, since he is now too weak to come to my office. Ruben will never stop fighting until his time has come, and he expresses gratitude to God for giving him nine years to see his children grow. He is an inspiration for many who know him and an inspiration to me.

Linda, thirty-four, from Ecuador, developed ovarian cancer that was metastatic on presentation and therefore unresectable. Despite her poor prognosis, she has lived for three years with this disease and I am sure that her strong faith and her love for life gave her this extended time. Linda was the single mother of two children. She told me many sad stories about her unsuccessful relationships with men. We became very close, particularly when the disease progressed to the point of requiring paracentesis every other day in order to relieve symptoms. During these times, we talked about our lives, our dreams, and our disappointments. She suffered from severe pain and chronic constipation. Her mother made her a cocktail of aloe vera juice from plants that she grew at home, and this is the only medication that seemed to keep her from obstructing.

Linda underwent multiple courses of chemotherapy and lost her hair several times, but always managed to make herself look attractive. She made the most of her beautiful green eyes and fair skin. In fact, the van driver who brought her to her appointments was in love with her, as were all the nurses in the office and the hospital. She read the Bible constantly and shared passages with me. One day, her friends from church came to the hospital to pray with her. I knew that the end was near, but she refused to accept this and prayed fervently for a cure. Because of her children, death was not a welcome possibility. She feared the influence of her ex-partner, who had married and moved away. While I was attending an out-of-town meeting, Linda developed respiratory distress and was eventually intubated. She died two days later, still believing that she would be cured. Her passing has left me with many beautiful memories, though I will always regret not being there at the end. I will never forget her strength or her courage.

My friend Guillermo has just passed away as I write this paragraph. He was seventy-two and had been a soccer hero in Peru some fifty years ago; he was a star on my mother's favorite soccer team. He even visited my mother in the convalescent hospital where she spent the last days of her life. In fact, Guillermo became so close that he listed me on his office intake sheet as a family member.

Guillermo sought my advice on every major decision that he had to make. After his fourth marriage failed, he was reluctant to take the plunge once again. I encouraged him to go through with it since I knew that the woman really loved him. He took my advice and his fifth marriage proved to be a success. At the time of his death, he had a teenage daughter from this last marriage, and children from previous marriages in various parts of the world.

Guillermo battled colon cancer for five years. He went into an initial remission, but he had rising tumor markers, although there was no identifiable source of disease, convincing me that he had relapsed. He received several courses of chemotherapy and his tumor markers decreased.

Fearing that his teenage daughter would become involved in gang activity, he bought a ranch and moved his family out of Los Angeles. He had once owned a ranch in Peru and had always longed to have the same in this country. He bought cows, ducks, and chickens, and raised cattle.

When his cancer recurred again, he went to another oncologist in his new community who gave him a new type of chemotherapy. The effects were devastating to Guillermo. He lost fifty pounds and developed severe diarrhea. After this, he resolved never to accept chemotherapy again. Although severe pain racked his body and tormented his mind, it became harder for him to afford his pain medications. Eventually, his pain became so bad that his wife had to take over the running of their ranch. About the time that Guillermo accepted placement in a hospice program, which provided him with free medication and unlimited home visits, his daughter moved to San Francisco to live with an aunt. He called me to intervene because his daughter refused to speak with him. I did my best, but she would not return my calls. Guillermo was heartbroken. He never stopped trying to reach her. He was still trying when I received the news today of his passing. His family was, is, and always will be the most important thing in his life.

Lucía, seventy-eight, from Colombia, was diagnosed with metastatic lung cancer. She presented with abdominal pain when I first met her and suffered this same pain for as long as I knew her. We became very close and I regarded her as one of my family. She spent many weeks in the hospital on account of chemotherapy-induced toxicity as well as for pain control. I learned much from Lucía—much about resignation when faith was the only thing left, about love for family and for the God who had given her so much love throughout her life. Initially, her family asked me not to tell her that she had incurable cancer. They felt that she was already profoundly depressed and that one more blow would be more than she could handle. She still grieved for her son who had disappeared five years earlier in the jungles of Colombia. I gently but firmly explained to the family that it was better to tell the truth because patients have the right to decide how they want to spend the last days of their lives. The family eventually agreed and allowed me to tell her.

But Lucía already knew the truth; she could sense it. In fact, she shared with me a dream that had occurred recently. She had dreamed of her death and, in fact, felt that she had for a brief moment died. She was surrounded by darkness but saw a light up ahead, as if at the end of a tunnel. She moved toward that light and felt an incredible feeling of peace and security that she had never felt before. That experience made her long to enter that tunnel once more, never to leave that light or peace again.

Lucía had always been a very intuitive woman. She knew what others were feeling and thinking, and passed this gift to her daughter and her granddaughter. We spent many hours talking about her family, her God, and her beloved son, whom she hoped to see again. During her final days, her sisters came from Colombia to be with her and to read the Bible to her. They also read from *Bioenergetics*, a book I recommended, written by a

Colombian doctor, Jorge Carvajal, who transformed his practice by incorporating his religious beliefs and his beliefs about man's role in the universe. She never lost her ability to smile, and we prayed together that God would take her to him soon to a place where she could rest without pain. At the end, she was too weak to talk anymore, but she could still smile. She died in peace with her family around her.

María is sixty-two years old and was born in Guatemala. She was diagnosed with colon cancer a year and a half ago and initially was sent for what we thought would be adjuvant chemotherapy. At the time of our first visit, it was apparent that she had already had metastasis to the liver. She received chemotherapy for over a year, and her tumor seemed to respond. Her disease eventually progressed, and she developed a pleural effusion that required chest tube drainage followed by talc poudrage. She later developed a severe vena cava syndrome with neck and facial swelling, for which she received radiation therapy. During this time, her tumor markers continued to climb. I explained to her that I did not think further chemotherapy would be of benefit, and I promised to maintain her in comfort with pain medication, oxygen, and whatever else she needed. I encouraged her to continue her prayer and to consider *uña de gato*, an herbal medication derived from a plant native to Peru, which many of my patients had found beneficial. On her next visit, she stated that she felt better, her facial edema had completely resolved, her pain was gone, and her appetite had returned. While her tumor markers remained unchanged, she clearly was doing better clinically. Whether the *uña de gato*, faith, or a combination of both was responsible, I cannot say. But she no longer fears the prospect of dying.

And finally, there is Marta, fifty-eight, diagnosed three years ago with breast cancer. After receiving adjuvant chemotherapy, she had relapse to her bones. She has not responded since her relapse to any chemotherapeutic regimen, yet she remains hopeful that she will conquer this disease. Her pain is quite severe and it has worsened recently, without metastatic spread to her ribs. She has been given radiation therapy, most recently Strontium 89 radioisotope, to control bone pain. In the meantime, her faith has given her the will to continue her struggle to overcome her trials. Someone at church gave her a tape about healing and a balm known as oil of Jerusalem. Since listening to her tape, applying her oil, and using a Fentanyl narcotic transdermal patch, she states that her pain has gone away and she is feeling much better. She is more at peace with herself as well.

Pain is common to all of my patients; control of pain is an integral part of oncology. Pain drains the spirit, robs the individual of hope, and leads to depression and, in some cases, suicide. Controlling pain allows patients to tap into their spiritual strength and their capacity to hope. Perhaps this is why the *curandero* is for many Latino patients more successful than traditional physicians in controlling pain symptoms. The rituals and ceremonies as well as herbal remedies integral to *curandero* give the patient a sense of control over the disease and thus hope for improvement.

I have seen many nurses and physicians attempt to remain uninvolved with their oncology patients. Those who manage to remain aloof often end up changing to another specialty, because pure clinical oncology can be very depressing and unrewarding. Becoming part of a patient's life is often the best reward our specialty has to offer, but can lead to burnout from overloading ourselves with the physical, emotional, and spiritual needs of others. I have found that the best insurance against burnout is to maintain our own support systems, whether this is through strong family relationships, strong spiritual commitment, or activities that take us away from our role as physicians.

I often share my own religious convictions with my patients. For those afraid to leave this world behind, I cite the Bible, where Matthew writes, "Do not store up for yourselves treasures on earth, where moth and rust destroy, and where thieves break in and steal. But store up for yourselves treasures in heaven, where moth and rust do not destroy and where thieves do not break in and steal. For where your treasure is, there your heart will be" (Matthew 6:19–21). For those in distress, Matthew says, "Who of you by worrying can add a single hour to his life?" (Matthew 6:25–27) Peter also says, "Cast all of your anxieties in God because he cares for you" (1 Peter 5:7).

My patients have taught me to understand that death is a part of life, a part that we cannot change, and a part that we must come to accept. They have taught me to live each day of my life as if it were the most important day ever. And finally, they have taught me that compassionate listening is a gift which becomes more valuable the more I use it.

La Quinceañera
Sweet Fifteen

Graciela Calatayud

A few days ago, as I entered my office, I was very glad to see a patient I hadn't seen in five years. My receptionist told me that Concepción wanted to be sure that she was going to be the first patient I saw as I arrived. As we walked down the corridor together, Concepción told me how happy she was to see me again. She had two small children with her, a little baby and a child of about one and a half.

"These are my sons," she said.

I was astonished. "How wonderful," I replied. "Let's talk a little more in private."

Let me tell you a little bit about Concepción. The first time that I saw her, she was very young, barely eleven years old. Her mother had just recovered Concepción from ten days of street life and had brought her in for a complete physical exam, to see if she had picked up a sexually transmitted disease. Concepción was very unreceptive about undergoing such an exam. She refused even to speak. I didn't insist on doing the physical exam, but spent a good forty minutes talking to her.

That first visit was the beginning of a series of constant visits, because Concepción was continually escaping from the house. Every time she returned, her mother brought her in for a visit. I didn't always do a physical exam; sometimes we would just sit and talk.

At first, I did all the talking; on some occasions, she did not utter a single word. But she led me to understand that she was not happy with life in her family, which consisted of her mother, her father, and a brother about two years older. Initially, she attended public school, where she was very influenced by her friends. Later, she enrolled in a private school but could not "find herself" there and, to a certain extent, forced her parents to let her return to the public school. This is where, I believe—and she believes as well—the pressure of friends to leave home began.

The mother worked, but after the problems with Concepción began, she quit working and dedicated herself to her daughter. However, Concepción continued to escape from the house, despite the fact that her parents drove her to school every morning and picked her up. She found opportunities to escape from school. Certain schools were very tardy in letting her mother know that she had not gone to school.

Little by little, Concepción became less involved in school and even less involved with her family. Concepción's friends kept begging her to participate in their various nighttime activities, which involved escaping from the house. Concepción participated in auto thefts, tire thefts, and car stereo thefts, and she began to drink heavily. She had her body tattooed, which her mother apparently did not notice.

Perhaps I should mention that Concepción is a very attractive girl with very fair skin, and she was well developed, even at eleven. She began to go out with men and began her sexual life when she was twelve years old. She insisted that she had only one boyfriend, so it wasn't necessary to do a physical exam every time her mother rescued her. The stream of visits from Concepción and her mother were real sob sessions—for her mother. Concepción's silence and difficulty gave her a certain amount of power. She felt that she could do whatever she wanted, that she could take care of herself, and that she didn't need the family, much less her mother. Concepción didn't want anyone to tell her what to do. On many occasions, the mother threatened to throw in the towel and send her to Mexico, as she had done with Concepción's older brother when he began to run in gangs. But she never did it.

At this point, as a result of her constant escapades, Concepción had established a relationship with a boy in prison. The mother was unable to do anything and the father was not much help. Finally, the mother acquiesced to this relationship, figuring that since Concepción now expressed no desire to escape, it was an improvement. So, when she was thirteen, Concepción married an inmate ten years older than she was. Although Concepción referred other adolescents to me who reported that she was more centered and seemed to have a purpose in life, I had lost contact with Concepción until a few days ago, when I saw her again in my office.

After Concepción left her children in the waiting room with her husband, she came back to the exam room, where we were alone. She hugged me very, very tightly, which pleased me and made me glad to have been so patient with her on previous visits. Suddenly, she began to cry.

Concepción told me that after her marriage, she began to see things a little bit differently. She wanted to continue her education. She became pregnant. She had to shoulder the responsibilities of motherhood and realized that she needed to spend time with the small society she had created with her husband and child.

It appeared that a doctor had diagnosed her husband with cirrhosis and told him that his liver was almost completely destroyed. She didn't know exactly what cirrhosis was or what was going to happen. We began to talk, and I explained the causes of cirrhosis, what happens, and what the most normal, natural course of this illness is.

Concepción began to cry again. She said, "Now that I have achieved a certain balance in my life, now that I have my sons, now that I have a husband who cares for me and we are trying to move ahead and better ourselves, this has to happen to us. My husband is very young and so am I! What is going to happen to us?" I took her by the hand and began to explain what the possibilities were, given her husband's age. It was quite likely, I explained, that he could have a liver transplant and a full life ahead of him. We talked for quite some while about the future possibilities. She called her husband in and I repeated the explanation to him: the causes of cirrhosis, the consequences, the prognosis, and what they could do for the time being. I referred them to the Organ Transplant Program at UCLA. We gathered as much information as we could for them, which they took when they left. For the rest of that morning—in fact for the rest of the day—I kept thinking about Concepción and remembering the first time I had seen her, when she was so young.

Back then, Concepción suffered very much, partially because of her immaturity, and partially because she wanted to. Her family wasn't what I would call dysfunctional, but perhaps Concepción, her brother, and the society in which they lived, in South Central Los Angeles, made it dysfunctional.

If there isn't internal solidarity in the family, adolescents get carried away by the strong social currents of life in gang-infested areas like the one Concepción and her family lived in. It is difficult to fight against this. I have seen it happen many times, particularly with young girls. The way they dress, the way they talk, with whom they talk. If they don't go along with the gang or with social groups in the school, then it becomes difficult to lead a normal life outside the house.

It is very difficult for a family with low income and limited resources—or even with medium income—to leave the South Central area where there is so much gang life. I understand this perfectly. But how do we help them?

Perhaps we can help by creating more social groups as alternatives for these children. Perhaps we could facilitate more participation of the parents, particularly the fathers, in the family. Perhaps we could form some community groups so there would be a counterbalance to this tremendous gang influence.

Religion often provides such an opportunity. It promotes a healthy interaction between adolescents and their parents and provides alternative gathering places, which can help fight against the tremendous gang influence.

However, as I have seen, school is often where the problem begins. Gang members or wannabe gang members either accept or reject students as soon as they enter the school and make life impossible for those who don't conform. It is difficult for adolescents to fight against this desire for acceptance and fear of rejection unless there is a strong family solidarity. And this is very, very difficult in communities such as South Central L.A., where both the mother and the father have to work many hours just to earn minimum wage to cover housing, food, and clothing.

Concepción, in her earlier visits, described to me what she had to do to become a gang member. They made her submit to sexual relations on various occasions. She also mentioned how she had to change her clothing, and even her makeup. At that point, the code demanded black lips, long hair, and shaved eyebrows.

But Concepción assured me that the gang members understood her. They were there for her. They accepted her. The gang members weren't always trying to tell her what to do. Everything that she did was accepted. In contrast, in her own home, everything she did was wrong, and she distorted the suggestions of her parents, especially her father.

As a pediatrician, I should mention that this period of adolescence is a time when children naturally begin to separate from their parents, and conflicts are exacerbated by the child's rising hormonal level, beginning around ten or eleven years of age. It is even more difficult if there is not a close relationship between parents and adolescents. Inevitably, the adolescent finds someone outside the house who says "everything that you do is okay. We accept you." But inside the house, the mother is always saying "Don't wear makeup like that. Don't dress like that. Don't talk like that." The child begins to think that she is being rejected and begins to rebel.

As this happened to Concepción, she began to like the changes in herself. She began to dress as her friends did. When her mother forbade her to, things began to change—even though the matter of dress is relatively insignificant. Concepción began to separate herself from her parents and to find herself more and more at home with her friends. They made her feel part of a family—a gang family. The gang members began to pressure her, but she didn't realize it until much, much later. And it wasn't until later that she realized the value of a real family.

I have seen cases where a teenager sometimes can take years to go through this evolution, but eventually they realize that they have to change. I have some patients who mature quite rapidly, sometimes as the result of parenthood, and I have others who still have not realized it. I have patients who are thirty-five or forty years, who still want to have a party life and be irresponsible, particularly in relation to the family. They want to have babies but have someone else raise them. They want to continue living as if they were single.

But I think Concepción is a very good illustration of what it is like to be a young girl growing up in South Central Los Angeles. At times she lived in abandoned houses, at times in friends' houses when the parents had no idea that their children had guests. She had sexual relations in houses that she didn't even know. She began to use different drugs, but she reassured me that she never injected them and that she only used marijuana from time to time. She was in juvenile hall a number of times, but she was never found guilty of the crimes that she had participated in. Still, her family had to suffer quite a bit before their daughter accepted responsibility for herself.

This is just one of many examples of young girls who finally leave gangs. And they do suffer. Not all of them achieve the level of maturity that I have seen in Concepción. She is now back in school, studying computer programming; she and her husband want to get ahead. Concepción has a certain pride and has developed a very positive outlook on life. She and her husband have achieved a family stability that isn't easy, demanding that they abandon drugs, abandon gang members, move out of prison life, and put it all behind them.

I think the health care provider has a very important part to play in the family dynamic. The provider is the first, often, to detect problems, particularly after long association with the family. As a pediatrician, I often have to instruct the parents from the very first visit about the importance of the relationship between the parents, particularly the father, and the child. I instruct them about the needs of the child, which change as the child grows. I tell them that this relationship is as important as eating and hugging. A child entering adolescence needs quite a bit of guidance and discipline. If the parents, or the family web, haven't established this discipline early, it is much more difficult to give it when the child is already an adolescent. Thus, as I see it, it is important for the health care provider to instruct the parents, especially young parents, about the future needs of the child, every time they visit. Doctor visits should consist of more than simply giving vaccinations.

In our Latino community, the mother is the one who does most of the work in providing this guidance and discipline. She is the authority figure. If the child does not turn out well, of course, she is the one who is given all the blame, though when things go well, the mother is given the credit, too. I emphasize to the young fathers the importance of their support for the mother and the responsibility of the father as part of this family web. I emphasize how important it is to have time specifically set aside for the children. It is not sufficient for the father just to come home and watch television, which is common. I strongly recommend that parents have at least one hour of quality time with the children, beginning from when they are very, very small. If this hour happens to be bedtime, then it is important for the fathers to say good night to the child, too. When the child sees that there is routine and discipline, it becomes a custom, and these customs gradually become family traditions. This is how one maintains a familiar solidarity.

As the child reaches adolescence, the parents, particularly the father, have to understand that the child doesn't necessarily have to adapt to the parents' wishes. The growing child's world changes and other things—dress, ways of doing things, music, games—change, too. It is very important that the father, in particular, participates in these changes, but it can't begin in adolescence. In fact, at that point, the child will often see the father or mother trying to enter his or her lives as if they were spies. The child has already learned to live in his own private world, and a parent trying to enter, at that point, without having had this lifelong custom, is seen as an intruder.

Much of my understanding of family psychology was gained quite early in my career. I am from Baja California and did my medical training in Mexico. Part of that training, during a stint at a free, community-based clinic on the outskirts of town, involved following one child for an entire year, reporting on both physical and social health. Eventually I came to Los Angeles, where, after more years of study (including English!), I began my career. For the last two decades, I have been working in family practice in Huntington Park. I work jointly with my husband, who is also a physician from Mexico but who functions as a physician's assistant in this country. He sees adults principally and I see both adolescents and adults, especially women. We offer all kinds of services in our little clinic and this is quite fulfilling for us. We are well established here and, I feel, popular and respected.

We really try to understand our population by practicing medicine the same way we practiced it in our countries of origin. The majority of our clients are Mexican and Central American. In spite of working in a large city such as Los Angeles, we feel, on many occasions, as if we were in a small town. Our patients bring gifts to the clinic—chickens, juices, bread, whole meals, mementos from their travels, and items from different parts of the hemisphere. We have patients who come from San Bernardino, Moreno Valley, Riverside, Santa Barbara, and Santa Maria, not to mention cities at the outskirts of Los Angeles such as Lynwood, Wilmington, and Canoga Park.

It is gratifying that our patients feel so at ease with us. They invite us to their parties, to their *quinceañeras*, to their weddings. Of course, this means they also involve us in their personal problems. When patients divorce their first spouse, they bring us their second spouse and sometimes even their third and more. But our patients have made us participants in their lives and we feel we are part of their families. Of course, this has helped us expand our practice as far as we have. I honestly feel that Jorge and I have done, and continue doing, social work, and this really pleases us, for I believe that such social and psychological work is part of medicine. Becoming involved in the family, being part of the folklore of the population, being part of our society: this is how Latinos practice medicine.

Qué Grande Es el Hospital

This Hospital Is So Big

Ted Estrada

I have worked in the health care field all my life, and for the past twenty-five years I have been the administrator of two different hospitals in East Los Angeles, California, home to the largest urban concentration of people of Mexican ancestry outside of Mexico City. During the past two decades, the Latino population in Los Angeles has swelled due to high birthrate and immigration, and today there are Latinos here from every country in Latin America: from El Salvador to Cuba, Peru, Argentina, Colombia, and Chile. These immigrants come seeking new and better lives for their families by accepting, sometimes stoically, the challenges and opportunities this country gives everyone. Many of these pioneers become discouraged and return to their towns and villages, stretching from the Rio

Grande to the Strait of Magellan. But those who remain retain their beliefs, their superstitions, and their distrust in the practice of medicine in this country, which stems, in part, from the language barrier. In order to be successful in treating the Latino patient, U.S. health care workers must recognize and accept, with patience, the varied ethnic, folkloric, and sometimes seemingly pagan beliefs held dearly by Latinos.

As a hospital administrator, the most exciting and enlightening part of my workday is visiting with patients, many of whom speak only Spanish. This allows me to find out about them and gives me an opportunity to hear what they think of our services. For example, I recently walked into the room of a three-year-old patient in our pediatrics ward. Her very dark-skinned parents, who seemed quite apprehensive, were at her bedside. They spoke Spanish haltingly. They were, the father told me, from a village in the Mexican state of Oaxaca, and they were Mixtec Indians who spoke Mixteco (a language continuously spoken since about 800 BCE). Eager to learn more about them, I took the father aside, and when he looked at me suspiciously, I assured him that I had no interest whatsoever in his immigration status; my primary concern—and that of the hospital—was to make his little girl well. He told me he had been in Los Angeles about four years, working in a tire factory. He had recently returned to Oaxaca to bring his wife and daughter to Los Angeles. His daughter had been sick for about two weeks and after being treated unsuccessfully by a highly recommended *curandera*, they had decided, reluctantly, to take the child to a doctor. He said that in his village in Oaxaca, a doctor comes to see patients only once a month, so the villagers are treated by midwives, healers, and *sobadores* when the doctor is not around. Often, he said, the doctor never shows up. His opinion was that most doctors are not very good. Fortunately, his little daughter with the beautiful bright eyes recovered and several days later left our hospital with her loving parents, who soothed her by speaking to her in Mixteco, the language her ancestors spoke almost three thousand years ago.

The experience with these Mixtec parents provided me with some excellent teaching tools to educate my staff. First, these worried and concerned parents are no different from any parent worrying about a sick child. But these parents had never been in a hospital before and did not know why their child was in a mist tent or why she was receiving intravenous fluids. We needed, I told my staff, to carefully and patiently explain to the mother (who never left the child's side during the entire hospitalization) everything that was being done for her child. Most important, the mother was never to be asked to leave the room when treatment was given to the child. Seeing that we were informing her of everything, the mother seemed more at ease with the staff, and began to see them with less suspicion and more trust. Our efforts to inform the parents about their daughter's treatment and progress, and our sincere concern for their little girl's welfare, translated into cultural sensitivity. Ironically, speaking Spanish to the parents did not really accomplish our goal of linguistic sensitivity: there was no way I could learn Mixteco in four days!

I was raised in a small Texas town where my maternal great-grandmother was midwife to the Mexican population. I remember going with her on her rounds, when she checked the expectant mothers. I, of course, was made to wait outside while she saw her patients. I remember sitting on the porch listening to the cries and screams of the women in labor and then the cries of a newborn. What a mystery that was to me! My greatest thrill was carrying Buelita's big black medical bag, in which she carried her instruments. I don't remember any of Buelita's patients dying; all the deliveries were normal (I don't recall her ever doing a C-section). Years later, when I queried her about her fees, she told me she charged twenty dollars per delivery. Sometimes patients did not have money and paid her with hams, vegetables, or live chickens (which I also had to carry along with the medical bag), or whatever the family had. I guess it was from my experiences carrying my Buelita's medical bag that, early in life, I developed an interest in helping others by entering the health care field, which has been my life's work.

Early in my career as a hospital administrator, a young man was brought to our emergency room with a work-related traumatic amputation of the right arm. He was taken to surgery and then spent about ten days recuperating in the hospital. The day he was discharged, he came to see me. I thought he came only to thank me for what we had done for him. I was unprepared for the true nature of his visit. What he wanted, he said, was his arm. He said that when he died, he wanted his arm to be buried in the same grave with him, in his village in Mexico.

I did not know what to say. Except for gallstones, which are sometimes given to patients, no removed body part ever leaves the hospital. The young man was calm but adamant. He said that when his grandfather lost his leg in a hunting accident, the leg was taken to church for a burial Mass—and then buried. Any part of your body, he explained, also has part of your soul. I was at a loss to respond. There was nothing I had learned in Anthropology 304 or Ethnology 402 that could help me here.

I told him, in Spanish, that in this country health regulations prevented us from giving him the arm. First, I said, it had been sent to the laboratory for study. "To study what?" he asked. "To look for findings," I replied. "What findings?" he again asked. "To see if everything was fine with the arm," I replied. "I never had any problems with it," he said. I could see I was getting nowhere. I told him that even if I could give him his arm, he would never get it through customs and onto the airplane. He said he would pay a *coyote* to smuggle it into Mexico. I told him to give me a few days to see what I could do, but I could not guarantee I could give him his arm. After he left my office, I could not believe this was happening to me after only three weeks on the job.

When I discussed the patient's request with the hospital's pathologist, I thought he would never stop laughing. First of all, he said, the arm had been dissected and was now in a large container of formaldehyde. Second, law requires we keep the specimen for seven years in case there is a future inquiry, after which time the specimen is incinerated. "Tell him," the pathologist said, "that in seven years we can give him the ashes." "You don't understand," I said. "This man believes we have a part of his body that requires burial in the same grave he will be buried in when he dies. He also believes he will not be whole if he is buried without his arm." The pathologist said there was nothing he could do, and added, "You have the authority to give him the arm, but I would not recommend it.

I must have been living right, or my guardian angel was carefully watching over me, because two weeks went by and the young man never called. I agonized during those two weeks, because I did not know what I would say when he did. How could I explain to a person who held strong beliefs about the soul that health and legal regulations prevented me from giving him back a part of himself? In retrospect, I'm glad the young man never called, because I might just have given him his arm. Who was I to keep it from him?

I have found that many Latinos hospitalized for the first time in their lives in the United States see hospitals with awe, suspicion, and sometimes fear. Many believe that they will not come out of a hospital alive, because they have had relatives or friends die in hospitals. Others believe that U.S. hospitals do not understand the Latino need for reassurance. Clearly, the U.S. hospital industry has not geared itself to deal with the customs, taboos, and beliefs of the Latino patient. First of all, many Latinos do not understand English. Some hospitals—even in areas like Southern California—have few, if any, employees who speak Spanish. I know a hospital in Orange County where maids and janitors are called from their duties to act as translators. How does someone with a limited knowledge of English explain or translate such things as advance directives, informed consent, and conditions of admission? Until U.S. hospitals in areas that serve Latinos make a true effort to establish policies mandating cultural and linguistic sensitivity for the Latino patients they serve, Latino patients will always be haunted by an aura of suspicion and apprehension about being hospitalized here.

I recently read through the standards of the national organization that accredits hospitals and found only one line suggesting cultural sensitivity. Nothing is mentioned about linguistic sensitivity or the need for all documents patients sign to be in a language the patient can understand. This organization is responsible for recommending quality assurance to all hospitals that submit to its accreditation scrutiny. I firmly believe these organizational reviews, scrutinies, and surveys must perforce mandate that U.S. hospitals demonstrate language and cultural sensitivity in order to provide the highest-quality care for their patients. To do otherwise is a travesty of the trust the patient places in the hospital and its medical and ancillary staffs.

The mores of the Latino are never more evident than when a loved one dies. Latinos, more than any other ethnic group I know of, is extremely clannish when relatives die. Every member of the family wants to be there. In one particular case, when a grandmother was dying from cancer, relatives came from everywhere in Mexico. They would not leave the hospital; the vigil was constant, intense. They would take turns sleeping, but there was always a group by her bedside, some praying, some crying. When the end came, it was utter despair: their grief was so intense we had to ask them to move into empty rooms because their lamentations were scaring our other patients. I know a hospital where, in a similar situation, the police were called to remove the grieving relatives from the hospital premises. Perhaps this was due to ignorance. Someone just did not know that we Latinos take the loss of a loved one with a grief so intense that almost nothing assuages it. The Latino spirit says, In my moment of unrelieved grief and sorrow when my beloved grandmother has just died, give me a room to cry in—but don't call the police.

Another important consideration in treating the hospitalized Latino patient is the matter of food. Early in my hospital administration career, I remember a dietary manager reporting that many of the trays served to patients were returned with the food hardly touched. Were all the patients so sick they couldn't eat? No plausible answer was given. The next day, I visited patients (most of whom were Latino) at mealtime and inquired about the food. One patient, from El Salvador, said she had never eaten mashed potatoes and broccoli before. Couldn't she have *caldo de pollo* (chicken soup) with fresh cilantro in it? Another patient asked if his wife could bring him *tacos de carnitas* (pork tacos) from a nearby taco stand—where I frequently saw hospital staff, including the dietitian, eating lunch.

The following day, I met with dietary, nursing, and social services personnel and several physicians. I told them that cultural sensitivity for our Latino patients had to include the type of food we served and that, contingent on what the physician ordered, we should involve the patients in planning their menus and serve them food they were used to eating. To our delight, within a few days of initiating our new program, patients were reported to be eating all their food. I received many compliments from patients and relatives about the changed menus and happily shared them with the staff members who, dedicated to providing our patients with the highest-quality care, readily supported my initiative.

In the history of medicine, the greatest physicians—Hippocrates, Galen, Avicenna, Chisdai ibn Shaprut, Maimonides, Joseph Lister, Ramón y Cajal—all agreed on one thing: besides your skill, the patient needs the reassurance that you truly want to help. Caregivers can best demonstrate their concern by showing sensitivity to patients' cultural, linguistic, and religious preferences, thus assuring the peace of mind so vital to the healing process. This dictum has held true through the ages, and is more important than ever in our multiracial and multicultural society.

Imagine you are from a remote village in any Latin American country. You have never been in a hospital. Suddenly, you are hospitalized in Los Angeles, Houston, Denver, or Chicago. People whose language you do not understand surround you. They ask you, using sign language and halting Spanish, to disrobe. They stick needles in your arm. They put you in a tube that takes pictures of what's inside your head (will it show what you're thinking?), they wheel you into a room where everyone wears masks and gloves. Slowly a mask descends over your face. The room starts spinning; you become very sleepy. And then.... Had enough? By now, some readers might be saying, "What hyperbole!" Then try this: Some years ago, a patient came into our emergency room with abdominal pains. The emergency room doctor found that he had a scar running from just below the sternum to the belly button. All the patient knew about this scar was that ten years before, having similar abdominal pains, he had been admitted to the emergency room of a large county hospital. When he woke up, the scar was there. He did not know what had been taken out (or, as he believed, what had been put in) or what had been done to him because, during his hospital stay, only those who cleaned his room spoke Spanish.

To this day, that man does not know what the scar on his body represents, because no one bothered to tell him in a language he could understand. As they say, there but for the grace of God go you or I.

Perhaps the Latino, in his wonderment and awe, does say of U.S. hospitals: *Qué grande es el hospital*. And with good reason. The hospital has cavernous halls, sanitized rooms, strange-looking tools and apparatuses that can look into the innermost parts of your body, documents to sign that only ten lawyers understand, and food that lacks all the flavors you love. They have few, if any, employees who speak your language.

The Latino is here to stay. Academicians and experts tell us the U.S. Latino is a multi-billion-dollar buyer of goods and services, including health care. U.S. hospitals need to take cognizance of and be sensitive to the Latino buyer, with all the attendant required sensitivities. Until then, we can only say—in the words of a song I recently heard—"What a wonderful world it will be."

No Ofendas

First, Do Not Offend

Camilo Jorge

I was born and educated in the Dominican Republic. I come from a family of doctors: I have a brother, some cousins, and various nephews practicing medicine. My parents were Lebanese immigrants who felt that each family had to have at least one doctor and one lawyer. I have been practicing in Los Angeles County for over fifty years, and most of my patients—probably 75 to 80 percent—are Latino.

I have been seeing some of my patients for fifty years, some of whom come to me from 200 miles away. I feel that I have been a successful practitioner because I treat my patients as family and take the time to understand them. It is my conclusion that a doctor who does not take the time to know his patients psychologically will not be a success with Latino patients. In my practice, my watchword has always been *no ofendas*—do not offend.

I hope that the patients who arrive at my door see what I see or, at least, would like to see: a physician who works humbly

with his patients, who offers all that he can to protect the
health of each and every patient. I try to give service twenty-
four hours a day, seven days a week. If a patient cannot afford
to buy medicines, I will make arrangements to provide it. I have
done this all my life, and my patients know this. They talk to
each other and tell each other about their visits to me.

In my experience, Latino patients will follow a doctor's
instructions to the letter if—and this is a big if—the physician
knows how to work with them. If the physician approaches a
Latino patient with arrogance, the patient will likely not follow
instructions and will probably not return.

Some patients cannot be treated solely by medications, but
have to be treated with psychology, with diplomacy. If not so
treated, they will never get better. I have to determine early
on if the patient comes in with a physical ailment, or a more
psychological one. A great number of the patients who come
to my office exhibit psychosomatic symptoms, usually what
they call *nervios*, often the result of the worries and stresses of
their lives. I have found Latinos quite open about sharing these
psychological woes with their physician; they hide very little. It
has been my good fortune that patients talk to me with frankness and don't hide things.

Just today I had one such experience. A little girl, just thirteen, came to me. She was pregnant and didn't want her parents
to know. But she readily confided in me. And I, as a physician
and a father, knew what to do and what to tell her. When she
left, she was reassured, and I felt that she wanted to do what I
had recommended to her. Her confidence in me was, I am sure,
in part because I have been treating her family for over thirty
years. In fact, I was the physician who attended her grandmother when her mother was born.

Yet, when I am treating a situation like this one, which has
many emotional ramifications, I have to be very careful how I

approach it. I work with the mother first. I prepare her with the information and let the parental roles take their course. The mother is the one who will tell the father. Of course, he might get angry at first; he might blame the mother for everything in spite of the fact that he might have a share of this "blame." But, in my experience, Latina mothers usually know how to communicate sensitive topics with the fathers.

I have to know my patients individually, so I can know how to treat each one differently. If I see that I can speak very directly and frankly with a patient, I get right to the point. But if I see that they are not open to that, I have to be more cautious and very diplomatic. The physician must consider each patient independently—no two are alike. Some will be reserved, of very few words, others are talkative. Some enjoy humor, others are dead serious. Therefore, to be a good physician, one also has to be a good psychologist. For, if the physician does not know how to approach the patient to broach sensitive topics, there is very little chance that the patient will be able to arrive at a true healing.

First of all, the physician has to listen to the patient. If a patient comes into the office and begins to complain, "I have this pain here and another over here and still more over there," the physician might suspect psychosomatic pain. However, there may well be a medical problem wrapped inside these psychosomatic symptoms. The physician has to know how to work his way through the psychosomatic problems to get to the medical ones. This is how I see my job.

I apply psychological skills to each patient to determine if the problem is strictly psychosomatic or if there is any additional medical problem, and in either case, what approach I ought to take. In a Latino patient base, there will be many patients who come in with largely psychosomatic, rather than medical, problems. But being psychosomatic does not make their concerns any less real, or any less important.

And there are psychological complications to clearly medical problems. I had one patient come to see me in a very depressed state. At first I thought his condition was only depression. But as I sat and talked with him, the medical issue emerged: there was something wrong with his penis. Many Latinos, particularly Mexicans, would rather die than lose their potency. He considered his life practically over.

It is not uncommon to see such pessimism in Latino patients, who feel that nearly any illness might lead to death. I have seen cases of pneumonia where the patient was ready to call in the priests for last rites. My biggest medical challenge was to convince this man that he was not going to die.

Another situation that calls for a delicate approach concerns the Latino sensitivity about modesty. About 80 percent of my patients are Latinas. In the realm of obstetrical care, they would really prefer to have a female physician attending a birth. This is because of their feelings of modesty, which they learned from their families. It is practically impossible to get an eighty-year-old woman into the stirrups for an examination by a male doctor. So what do I do?

Whatever it takes, the most important thing is to gain her confidence. Often, I can accomplish this through humor. "I'm going to find a husband for you," I might joke with this octogenarian. But what works in this case might not work for everyone. What matters most is that the physician takes the time to find the correct approach.

I know that patient compliance can be difficult to obtain. Some physicians think that if they scare patients, or nag them, they will achieve compliance. But this has not been my experience. Let us suppose we have a hospitalized patient announce that he wants to leave the hospital this very instant, even though it is not medically indicated. An inefficient physician might try to scare the patient, saying, "If you leave today, you are going to lose that foot." Another might argue with the patient: "I am the doctor and I know better."

In such a case, I would go to the patient's bedside and try to find out what is really going on. I might say, "Señor Bonifacio, if you want to leave, I cannot make you stay, but I would like you to come to my office first thing. Even though you might not believe it, I know that you have a cancerous tumor." Then he might reply, "I know that. I want to leave because I do not have any more money." Now, we are coming to the real problem: he does not feel he can afford any more services. I would tell him, "I know that you want to check out because you don't have money, but your care is the hospital's responsibility. And besides, if you leave, think of the problems you will impose on your family! They do not know how to care for you like the nurses here do. Let the nurses do their job." Finally, I would talk with the nurses, with the administration, with other doctors, and make arrangements so that the patient could be seen without worrying about the burden of payment.

Seeing seventy to eighty patients a day, I feel I can speak with confidence about what works with Latinos in general. My experience is that Latino patients are very expressive verbally, though of course this is not the case with all. I have learned that I have to be as expressive as they are. For example, if I want a woman patient to lose weight, first I compliment her on her qualities, then build on that. I have never had a woman patient feel offended when I tell her, "Look, you are a very attractive woman. If you want to look even better, you might lose a little weight."

Humor works with men, too. For example, one patient was a baker with a liver problem who would not quit drinking. I can tell him, "Man, you're killing yourself." But if I really want him to quit drinking, I tell him he is killing himself and will leave his children without a father. "Yes, Doctor, for my children I'll stop drinking," he will reply. Latinos generally take their social obligations—the role of mother, father, wife, husband—very seriously. I achieve this result by touching on this important obligation.

In all these examples, the underlying principle, the most important thing I have learned in my practice, is this: *no ofendas*. This leads me to the subject of alternative healing methods. Many of my patients use herbal remedies. Personally, I do not accept such use, but neither do I deny it. I respect their treatments just as I respect chiropractic treatments. I would never say, "Stop using those herbal remedies," for this would not get me anywhere. Because of my attitude, patients don't hide from me the fact that they are seeing *curanderas*. One patient with kidney stones was treating himself with chamomile tea, then smoking marijuana because of the pain. I told him, simply, "Señor, these herbs may feel good, but they will do nothing to get rid of that stone. Let's see if we can find a way to take care of it."

Dealing with death is always delicate for a physician. Following my lifelong practice of courtesy and respect, I never tell a patient outright, "You are going to die." I feel that it is important that patients never lose hope, and if you tell them they are going to die, they may lose hope and die even more quickly. Their death kills some portion of their family. If I have a patient with a cerebral hemorrhage, we sit down, have a cup of coffee, and converse. Gradually, we talk about the different things that might happen. I feel that if I take away hope, I am taking away life, little by little. Instead, we talk about the possibilities of cures, of new forms of medical research, of miracles.

I have always been conscious that Latino patients, especially Mexican patients, see the doctor almost as a god, if they feel that there is a sense of confidence. Although physicians are highly educated, not all are what Latinos would call *educado*. Some are incapable of offering their hand to a patient. Yet there should be complete confidence between patient and doctor because of the delicate subjects that must be touched on. I have noticed that some non-Latino physicians seem to feel that Latinos are servile beings who can be humiliated and insulted into compliance. This attitude never works. Immigrant Latinos are very humble, obedient, responsible, and grateful, but never servile. When some of my older patients, who I know have very little money, bring me a plate of tamales out of gratitude, it touches my heart, and I feel that I have done my job well.

La Mujer
Woman

Margarita Keusayan

I was born and raised in the small South American country of Uruguay. I grew up in the capital city, Montevideo. Throughout my childhood, I watched my country, once called the Switzerland of South America, degenerate into one of the poorer countries in the southern cone. Even so, Uruguay maintained its high social standards, in both literacy and education.

As the firstborn of an Armenian couple who had emigrated at the turn of the century, I soon learned the difficulties and challenges of superseding my forefathers in economic well-being and education. One day, at the age of fourteen, while studying for my physiology class, I discovered the perfection and complexity of the human body, which ignited my passion for knowledge and spurred my study of the human body and its functions. Despite racial and sexual prejudice and economic hardship, I devoted my youth to my studies and eventually I entered the University of the Republic of Uruguay. It was 1958 when I first walked into the halls of the university.

Ten years later I walked out with the MD that many said was unobtainable by a woman. It came at a high price: years of hard work and dedication. But in those final years of internship and residency at the University Hospital, I learned the important human skills required to interact with the patient, which complemented the knowledge I had acquired from books and professors.

Those years gave me the insight to see the difference between the doctor and the patient: two human beings, one in need and vulnerable, the other empowered to give and seemingly omniscient.

After several years as an emergency room physician and in private practice, the quest for knowledge and growth, which had been with me since adolescence, demanded that I explore new and unfamiliar pathways. So, in 1972, with two children and a third on the way, my husband (also a physician) and I packed our belongings and moved to the United States.

Drawing a parallel to my forefathers who had immigrated to Uruguay, I soon learned what it meant to study, work, and live in a foreign country. Adjusting to the United States was not easy, but in 1976 I became a licensed MD and completed all the requirements that enabled me to practice medicine once again. I realize that those difficult years helped me progress, not only in terms of my career but also in my ability to treat Latino patients with respect and prudence.

In 1987, I opened my private medical clinic in the heart of the Latino community of Los Angeles. Little did I know that ten years later, this small clinic would be serving so many underprivileged men, women, and children. The tremendous growth of the practice has been due to several factors. Success in the field not only is determined by being a good physician but also requires reaching into the heart of the people and understanding their culture. I like to say that I become part of the patient;

I feel the patient's anguish and share in his suffering. But it does not stop there. I become part of the patient's family and environment. This has proven to be a learning experience, since no two patients are alike.

The forty years that I have been a physician have helped me grow personally, but more important, they have enabled me to give something back to the Latino community in which I was raised. I would like to share with you several real cases that, I hope, will demonstrate how and why I am successful in reaching these people.

A sixteen-year-old female came in by herself for a consultation about a delayed menstrual period. When the positive result of the pregnancy test came in, she burst into tears. I was taken aback by her immediate outburst. But she soon composed herself and requested a termination of the pregnancy.

I asked about her circumstances, and it was immediately clear that she had a stable relationship with the father and she also had sufficient financial means to support this child. Even though it was a frightening and unplanned event, she appeared to want to keep the child, but felt she could not. So, I made a deal with her: wait twenty-four hours. Sleep on it for that night. When she came in the next day, she had decided that she and her boyfriend would keep the baby. The pregnancy and delivery were uneventful. A healthy baby girl was delivered.

Two years later, she came in for prenatal care for a second pregnancy. Her relationship with her partner had developed and they had married. The second pregnancy was also uneventful, with regular prenatal care visitations. Currently, she, her husband, and their two children are patients of mine. She still remembers the turmoil of her unplanned pregnancy and fears what she might have done had she not been treated with prudence and care.

This is a case of a nineteen-year-old female patient who came in with her infant baby for consultation. The young woman had a twenty-four-hour history of fever on and off, nonquantified, occasional vomiting, nausea, and abdominal pain. After examination, it appeared to be a clear case of acute appendicitis. After explaining the condition, the prognosis, and the treatment plan, the patient understood that immediate hospital admission was required. To my surprise, she agreed to first drop off her infant baby at home.

I made all the necessary preparations, including advising the surgeon of the pending appendectomy. Seven hours later, with everything ready to go, the patient had not shown up at the hospital. At that point in time, I did not expect her to appear. On the eighth hour, she presented herself at the hospital for the procedure. Her condition had now deteriorated into acute peritonitis.

Inquiring about the delay, I was told that she had spent those critical hours in search of a babysitter and trying to get in contact with her husband. She had no means of transportation. Her devotion to her child was far more important than her own condition. I will always remember this experience because it made me change my handling of similar situations. Now, I demand that patients go to the hospital, and I verify every aspect of that order.

This is the story of a very sweet and loving woman, seventy-six, who is a regular patient at my clinic. She came in for physical checkups and would occasionally come in for seasonal allergies. She had no other major medical problems. As Christmas approached in 1994, she came in looking for advice. She wanted to visit her hometown; she hadn't seen her son in the twenty years since she had left. Considering her general good health, I okayed the trip. I refilled her allergy prescription and wished her bon voyage and the best for the holidays and her upcoming family reunion.

In March of the following year, she came back to my office and I could immediately see that she had changed. She had come in with a friend who understood that she needed immediate medical attention. When I asked what the problem was, she began to cry. Her friend explained that the Christmas trip back home had disrupted her life. Upon her arrival, she was unable to function as she previously had. Her friend explained to me that she had spent the majority of her visit crying. She was emotionally distraught because of problems between her daughter-in-law and her adored son.

Once I made the diagnosis of a major depressive episode, I referred this patient to a psychiatrist. For two years, she continued to return to my clinic to let me know how she was doing while in her group psychotherapy sessions and with her medication. At the end of this treatment, she was discharged and came back under my care. To my surprise, she again planned to go back to her hometown to visit her son. I could hardly believe my ears.

I quickly shifted my role with this patient from medical doctor to counselor, even therapist. I strongly urged her to write a letter to her son to explain what she had gone through since her last visit. This did not seem to satisfy her emotional needs. It took me a while to convince her to write to her son and forgo the visit, but in the end she agreed. I was finally content and felt that I had prevented a possible disaster.

* * *

Margarita Keusayan passed away on October 20, 2000, after a fourteen-year battle with breast cancer. She was sixty-one years old. She had outstanding courage and a determined spirit in her fight against this terrible disease.

As her daughter, and her physician assistant, I witnessed her daily struggles personally and professionally. Doctora

Margarita didn't live for herself; she lived for others—for her patients, for family—and to practice medicine. Helping to heal, she found her calling, extended her health, and found a truly meaningful life.

At forty-seven years old, she discovered a lump in her breast. She had an immediate radial mastectomy, and it was found that her cancer had spread. The surgeon informed her in a matter-of-fact tone that the prognosis was not good. He advised her to stop working and to start making appropriate arrangements.

This was not acceptable news! She was a doctor! How could this happen? For the first time in her life, the doctor was to become the patient. What did she do? She fought a full-fledged war against breast cancer.

She was diagnosed when I was fifteen years old. We didn't think she would live to see me graduate high school. Not only did she see me do that, but she also saw me graduate UCLA and Charles Drew University, get married, give birth to two children, and take over her medical practice.

Doctora Margarita was a person who truly enjoyed life. She had an infectious laugh, one that took up the whole room—a really big laugh, deep, full-hearted, and bursting. She made the most of the moments she had and so did we. She used the diagnosis of breast cancer as a reason to really live life and enjoy it.

Two years after her diagnosis, and in between her radiation and chemotherapy, she opened a new practice in the largely Latino city of Cudahy. She was the only female medical doctor in the area. Her patients did not know she had breast cancer, although most probably suspected that she was in ill health. But Doctora Margarita would not stay in bed. I think that was her secret. No matter how bad she felt, she had me pick her up and bring her to *la clínica*. At Clínica Santa Clara, somehow her cancer pain diminished. Practicing medicine, working, helping others, delegating, and being "*la doctora*" made her physical worries temporarily vanish. It didn't take long before news of the good female doctor spread. Everyone in Cudahy knows everybody else, and everybody is either related or compadres, therefore she was very popular.

She still has a large patient following. It is amazing how many patients need a mother figure and her "tough love." They definitely received tough love from Doctora Margarita. She kicked diabetics out of our office MANY times for confessing to eating pancakes *con miel* before an office visit. "Para qué vienen al doctor?" she screamed at them as they left in disbelief. She asked patients who didn't take their blood pressure medication whether they preferred to die from a heart attack or a stroke. With Doctora Margarita it was not *what* she said, it was the *way* she said it. She was stern but caring, authoritative but not condescending. If she was yelling at a patient—which she did often—that patient understood that it was because she was genuinely concerned about their health.

Grown men still cry remembering their beloved doctora. There are other patients who have told me their dreams in which my mom spoke to them about their personal struggles. For some, she was their only counselor and confidant. Still other patients have told me about altars they built in memory of their doctora. Her presence had a vast impact in the small Latino community of Cudahy.

She practiced medicine for the love of it and truly tried to help her patients. As the years go by, I feel I am continuing her legacy—Doctora Margarita's legacy. A patient told me the other day, "I finally found a doctor who really cares about me!" I felt my mom's presence with me at that moment.

Leticia Keusayan Gonzalez, PA-C

Silence

Luz Dillary Diaz

On her face were the dry wrinkles of experience. Her eyes were full of maternal tenderness; her look was lost in the distance. On her head was a scarf of a reverential age. In the cold neon light of the quiet white room, she seemed unassailable. And indeed, I did not know how to approach her.

How much would she know? What would she have been told? Who had translated the doctor's news?

I opened the door. "My name is Luz and I am at your service. What do you know about what has happened?"

"The doctor says that there is no more hope, that our son is dead and that the machines are just keeping him alive."

"What happened?"

"The doctor said that they found him lying down, that somebody reported it to the police and called an ambulance. Somebody stuck a screwdriver through my son's head. I want to take him back to Mexico. He sends us money every month so we can live. He is a good son. He helps everybody. He only did good deeds. How can we take him back to Mexico? Can you help us?"

I opened my information folder. My hands were cold, my throat was dry. Hoping to provide relief for their pain, I presented a brochure with a toll-free 800 number.

My heart beat wildly, my pulse accelerated; I made the sign of the cross as if I were in the presence of God, not man. I prayed, and then I asked my question (as I write these lines, my hands tremble and I live each moment again).

"In your pain and suffering, I ask you to consider the possibility of helping others who wait and may die, hoping for an organ transplant. Have you ever heard of transplants?"

One more time, silently, I prayed: "In the name of the Father, the Son, and the Holy Spirit, I surrender, I ask for pardon and mercy from God, who has heard this request. God's ways are mysterious to us humans, while they are clear and precise to Him."

"No," said the mother. "We don't understand what you are talking about."

"I am talking about helping others in the memory of your son. About how, in an act of love and life giving, you can donate his organs so that others may live. You brought him into this world, gave him life, now you can help others by giving him a second chance to be born again."

The atmosphere was tense, suffocating. I didn't know what more to say; as a matter of fact, there was nothing more to be said. I came closer and squeezed their hands with mine.

"You must be experiencing great pain. I see so many sad cases, so much pain."

"It has not been easy," answered the father. "We made it to the border. The hospital sent a letter that would allow us to come across, but can you imagine—they denied us entry. What could we do? We had no choice. We had to cross. We hired one of those individuals who bring people across. They charged us a lot of money. It was very risky, but we made it. And what for? Our son had died."

Now what? I couldn't say anything more. In the presence of so much pain, how could I ask anything of them? How could I ask them to give up their son so someone else's son might live?

Silence…

Silence kept us together. Simple silence.

Finally, the father said, "Well, if it is going to help another, let it be."

Que Dios Guíe Sus Manos
May God Guide Your Hands

Ismael Navarro Nuño

*I*n the evenings, I often sit at my office desk, looking out my window at the city lights. These are moments of reflection on the past, on accomplishments, failures, and triumphs. From my office, I can see downtown Los Angeles. The city skyline, the noise, and the busy streets are an affirmation of life as I live it in this city. Sometimes it bewilders me that I have become a player in this drama. I think of myself as a child, born and raised in Tijuana, and my painstaking transformation into the chief of heart surgery at a well-known institution.

It has been a long and arduous road, a road of learning, experience, and hope. I have learned many lessons in life, and I have become a leader. Every day I take on the responsibility of life and death for my patients, who include the Latino pegs in the board of life in Los Angeles.

My practice is based entirely at the Los Angeles County–University of Southern California Medical Center (LAC-USC

Med Center). My office is located on the tenth floor of a monstrous shell of concrete built in 1929. Even though the hospital has more than a thousand beds, it is always overfilled and there are often patients in beds lining the halls. Along the main corridor of this institution, large pictures depict medicine at the hospital in the 1930s. Their dramatic presence provides a sense of continuity, yet shows me how far medicine has come.

The area demarcated for my open-heart surgery patients has two large ward areas, one each for males and females, with seven beds each, and one bathroom on each side. The intensive care unit of the ward has eight beds, fully equipped with state-of-the-art monitoring equipment. How modern technology functions in that early-century setting is an enigma.

I, too, am a mixture of the old and the modern. I was born in Tijuana to a family with very humble beginnings. My father and mother were originally from Guadalajara, Mexico. My three sisters and I were raised in a neighborhood just ten meters south of the international border. Our neighborhood housed prostitutes, drug dealers, and the poorest of the poor. But it was home to all of us, and we all respected each other's boundaries.

For the kids of the barrio, our version of "chicken" involved crossing the barbed wire separating the two countries to throw rocks at the passing *migra* patrol cars. He who ran away last, defying the *gringos*, became the neighborhood leader of the hour. Sometimes, I would grab a burlap sack and march into the fields on the U.S. side of the wire and pick fresh corn. My mother would cook the corn, and we would have a great feast for dinner that night. I had many happy moments, and many dreams, as I grew up in Tijuana.

Even as a child, I ran around taking people's blood pressure with my doctor's bag of toy medical instruments. I had an inexplicable fascination for the heart, the seat of the soul. One day in 1967, *Life* magazine showed pictures of the miraculous first heart transplant by Dr. Christiaan Barnard of Cape Town, South Africa. My life changed forever with that news. My goal in life was now to become a heart surgeon. I, too, would do such marvelous things with the heart. School would be a means to that end, and college would be the first dragon I would have to slay. Medical school, specialty training, internships would come later.

I completed my medical training in Guadalajara, my training in general surgery at the University of California at San Diego, and my training in cardiac surgery at the Walter Reed Army Medical Center in Washington, D.C. I saw service at the Presidio in San Francisco, California, and Heidelberg, West Germany. I became an assistant professor of surgery at the Uniformed Services University for the Health Sciences at Bethesda, Maryland. I saw various theaters of conflict, the most vivid of which was the Gulf War in 1990-91, where I was medical commander of the Fifth MASH.

When I departed from the armed forces, I taught cardiac surgery at the University of California at Irvine Medical Center. From there, I developed my practice in the Los Angeles area until I joined the staff at the University of Southern California, where I taught residents once a week at the LAC-USC Medical Center. Within a year, I became chief of the cardiac surgery service at the center.

I see patients of many different cultural groups in my practice, but Latinos make up approximately 75 percent of my patient population. Different cultural traits are easy to spot among this diverse group of people. As Latinos, we share certain cultural characteristics, among them humility and modesty, respect for authority and the elderly, belief in family unity with strongly established lines of hierarchy, unbendable religious convictions, and the perception that medicine in America is of the highest quality.

The patients who come to me for open-heart surgery, merely by being at high risk, are an unusual subset of patients. For most procedures, the operative mortality rate is 3 to 5 percent; for a straightforward hernia operation, for example, risk of death is extremely rare. But open-heart surgery is different. Discussions between cardiac surgeons and their patients and families have to be much more intense, honest, and at times morbid. Cultural perceptions about death become very significant.

Before reaching me, the heart patient, young or old, usually has been seen by a primary physician, an internist, and a cardiologist. At the beginning, my exposure to the heart patient is very narrow. My preoperative counseling conversation is brutally realistic. Logically and methodically, I explain the surgery to them. Invariably, the patient is told of the possibility that he or she may not survive the open-heart surgery. I tell them that the last kiss they give their children just before being rolled into the operating room suite may be the last time they touch each other. I tell the family that the day of surgery may be the last time they will see their loved one smile. I have noticed that the physical separation at the door to the operating suite is handled differently by various cultures. Asian families will be very quiet and handle the moment of separation with resignation and silence. Americans will usually shower the patient with kisses and tell them they will see them in a few hours; the expectation of success is always present. But in Latino culture, the family will invariably place the entire hope, fear, and responsibility on the surgeons. "Cuide mucho a mi papá, doctor. No deje que le pase nada malo. Que Dios lo guíe" (Take good care of my father, Doctor. Don't let anything bad happen. May God guide you).

It is very difficult for me, as a Latino and as a surgeon to my Latino patients, to be objective about what I say to them and how I say it. Many of the little Mexican ladies remind me of my mother; the elderly men remind me of my father. Everything—their style of clothing, their mannerisms, their beliefs—makes it personal for me. When one of my patients dies, it affects me very much.

Latino patients are generally very modest in their appearance and shy about exposing themselves to strangers. In the surgical ward, however, patients are placed in a room with six other patients. The room will be crowded by seven patients, their visiting relatives, four to six doctors, one or two nurses, and two or so aides. Though there are linen curtains surrounding each bed, realistically, all privacy and modesty are sacrificed. The difficulty of examining Latino patients in such a public setting is noticeable. At times, I have come across Latino patients who would rather die of their heart disease than give up their modesty. The public nature of this examination is the first hurdle these patients face on their journey toward healing, and it is usually met by their relatives with a joking phrase such as *que ranchera* (so shy).

At times, parents take on the responsibility of modesty for their children. The mother of a teenage Mexican girl I was about to operate on requested very emotionally that she be allowed to stay with her daughter day and night—including going to the operating room—so that she might make sure her daughter's body was not seen naked by male doctors and nurses. The mother's request was appropriately denied after a long, kind discussion was undertaken with her, during which she was reassured that a female nurse would always be with her daughter. Most of our nurses are of Latino origin, so they understood her concerns.

Obedience is another characteristic of many Latino patients, whether from Mexico, Central America, or South America. Latino patients will accept whatever is said or done to them. Rather than submission, this obedience shows respect. Culturally,

Latinos have been taught to respect the word of authority, and in the hospital, doctors and nurses are the authorities, right or wrong. As illogical as an order may be or as painful as it is to carry it out, the Latino patient will do it—no questions asked. When surgery is canceled because of other emergencies, they will accept their fate without complaining. The Latino patient would rather accept pain than question authority—it's just another day of waiting. "Es mi cruz" (It is my cross). When I tell patients that I will stop their heart for two to three hours to fix it, they accept the plan with resignation—"Aunque me cueste la vida, que le vamos a hacer?" (Even if it costs me my life, what am I going to do about it?) The respect for authority is absolute, even to the detriment of the patient or the family.

I once canceled the surgery for a sixty-year-old female patient from Michoacán, scheduled for coronary bypass. When I told her that I had to do an emergency operation on another patient, she looked up to the ceiling and very quietly said, "Válgame, Dios!" She did not want to overrule my authority even though she was having significant pain at the time. The pain and the possibility of losing her life were secondary to my authority. Had it not been for the EKG changes on her monitor, I would not have known of her distress. She would have continued in pain and might possibly have died. Her surgery was done very late that night, after the emergency surgery was completed. The patient did well, and eventually went home. Though her case turned out well, the total respect for authority so common to Latino patients might have cost this woman her life.

Latino patients, for the most part, understand, and believe in, the state-of-the-art technology for open-heart surgery in the United States. When they come to America and place their lives in the hands of American doctors, they do so with blind faith. Everything, and anything, within the confines of the hospital is equally important to them. The opinions given by the doctor, the nurse, the dietitian, the aide, and the janitor are all important and equally valuable—all a part of the institution that will save them. The lower the Latino patient is on the socioeconomic ladder, the more profound this belief is.

When I treat well-to-do patients from Mexico, I introduce myself in Spanish and tell them that I also am from Mexico. Sometimes, they become upset. "No vine desde Mexico para ver a un médico mexicano" (I did not come up from Mexico just to be seen by a Mexican doctor), they say. There are very real lines of demarcation in beliefs in different economic, social, and immigration strata. Generally speaking, first-generation Latino patients bring "old-world" traditions that should be considered by the physician. Second-generation Latinos, especially those who have attended college, whether patient or child of a patient, bring a more complete understanding of the complex problems of medicine and will often pose very focused and significant questions.

Strong family unity is also very much a Latino cultural trait. The Latino patient frequently comes to the clinic for the first time accompanied by various family members. Some come for support, others because they furnish transportation, others because they can translate from English into Spanish. Others are there because the patient wants to keep them close. Whether it's the outpatient clinic, an inpatient setting, or the ward, family presence will be constant. When the surgeon explains the procedure and prognosis to the patient, family members will be present. In fact, the patient will usually politely decline to even develop the conversation until the relatives are present. "Luego viene mi hija; ella sí le entiende, para que le oiga" (My daughter will come later; she will understand you, so she can listen to you). Questions will come from the family in hierarchical order, in order of seniority: first the husband, then the oldest son or daughter, then others.

On the morning of surgery, expect the family. If the surgery is at five in the morning, the family will be there. Other families may give a phone number in case there are any problems. The Latino family will accompany the patient to the last possible moment. They will very patiently and loyally wait immediately outside the operating room suite—the waiting room is too far away. The spouse, the children, the children-in-law, the grand-children will all be in attendance. As the surgeon comes out to greet them, the spouse and the oldest child will approach first. Everyone else will respect their position in the hierarchy of the family and stand back.

Children are as diverse as they are individual, but in my perception, there is a pattern. The children of first-generation Latino families are behaviorally indistinct from their parents. Second-generation children—especially those who may be attending college—are much more aggressive. Observation of hierarchy and obedience to authority, as shown by the older Latino patients, are less noticeable, and there are signs of new cultural influences, of modernity and of technical understand-ing. A sigh of resignation is no longer the cultural trademark of the new generation. Instead, smart young Latinos want answers to their questions.

As technology has advanced, traditional Latino beliefs have also been put to the test. The Latino patient believes that the character—kindness or meanness, astuteness, love, and passion—comes from the heart. What happens, then, to a patient who receives a heart transplant? Will the character change? Will Jovita lose her kindheartedness? When I coun-sel patients for possible heart transplant, their concern is not survival, but rather whose soul will live inside of them. (The same concern does not surface when these patients receive kidney or liver transplants.) Once the old and diseased heart of the patient is removed, these patients believe, the soul will also be lost: a totally new individual will emerge. So should we mourn the symbolic death of the patient at the time of the transplant?

The religious beliefs of the Latino patient population has always been an enigma to the residents that I train. After the patient is admitted, counseled, and prepared for surgery, the patient will invariably make a statement: "Estoy en sus manos y en las del Señor" (I am in your hands, and God's). The patient has complete and absolute belief in God Almighty's promise that everything will be all right. You, the surgeon, will be the instrument for that divine undertaking. Even so, it is not the surgeon but the surgeon's hands that will be the instruments of healing and miracles. "Que Dios guíe sus manos" (May God guide your hands). It is the perception of my residents that when the Latino patient says it is up to God, they are placing 100 percent of the responsibility upon them. In reality, the patient is not refusing responsibility but bestowing honor upon us. They are saying that the only other person they trust their life to, other than the young surgeon, is God.

After the surgery, love and admiration for the physician may be taken one step further and lead to adoption. The patient and the family may address the surgeon in a more friendly fashion. Respect and admiration for the surgeon is at its peak, and the family will have elevated you to the honorable position of family elder: "Usted ya es un miembro de nuestra familia." They will bring you home cooking as a show of their appreciation. One family brought my crew Mexican food every day of the week and would not eat until we had eaten. I kept getting invitations to their home and their family gatherings for years. Relations with Latino patients and their families typically will become long lasting. However, the truest test of affection and acceptance is when you are finally allowed to call family members by their first name.

Death is a very real part of the practice of open-heart surgery. Though the Latino family accepts that death is a natural passage of life, reaction to a death can vary with each family and each individual. Death from heart surgery is to be expected, and accepted should it happen. After all, the patient had surgery in the United States; if the surgery had been performed in Mexico or another Latin American nation, all of the current technology might not have been available.

After the death of a parent or sibling, Latinos are usually very demonstrative. Crying and outward show of pain is much more evident than among other cultures better known for their stoicism. The wife of a patient of mine who had just died in the intensive care unit after surgery was so distraught that she threw herself upon his body and kept wailing. After approximately five minutes of this, I tried to separate her from her husband's body. She yelled at me, "No sea tan cruel! Porqué me quieren quitar de aquí?" (Don't be so cruel! Why do you wish to take me away from here?)

In some cases, the belief in the power of their religion, their God, or a saint is so strong that death of a loved one may come as a complete surprise. Upon the death of one of my patients with a very ill heart, I walked into the hallway and told the patient's wife of her husband's death. As I was describing the events of the surgery, the poor woman took out a twelve-inch statue of Baby Jesus and starting yelling at it. "Me prometiste que me lo ibas a cuidar. Porqué me mentiste? Porqué me abandonaste?" (You promised me you would look after him. Why did you lie to me? Why did you abandon me?) I did not know whom to feel more sorry for—the patient who had just died, the poor wife, or myself.

It is clear that other cultures may share traits with the Latino patient in America. But it is the combination of these traits— and the extent to which the Latino patient is willing to risk life and limb to maintain those traits—that makes the Latino so unique. As a Mexican American heart surgeon, I, too, have many of the cultural traits I have described above. My modesty, my strong sense of respect, my obedience for authority, and my religion are all chips of the mosaic that forms me and the rest of the Latino culture. Just before I open the chest of a patient in the operating room, with my sterile-gloved hand I will make the sign of the cross over the patient's heart. When I lose a patient in surgery, I will go out and cry with the family. When all goes well and the patient goes home, I have become a part of their family and the patient has become part of mine.

A Gallon of Healing

Norbert Sharon

*T*his would be an incredible story if it weren't the simple truth. It didn't happen in the Middle Ages. Jacob lived from 1978 to 1997. Jacob's father, mother, and one sister died of cancer. When Jacob was eight, the doctor told him that he had cancer, too. His aunt began to cry. "Don't cry, Tía," Jacob said. "I'm going to be an angel!"

Jacob spent the next eight years in and out of hospitals. He had bone replacements and skin grafts; his left arm was amputated. But any time Jacob was not in the hospital, he managed to come to Mass and to Communion. Sometimes he came on crutches, sometimes in a wheelchair. Often he bravely limped up to the altar.

When I visited Jacob at City of Hope Hospital, he told me, "Father, the doctor just told me that there's no possible cure. I have cancer all over."

"Are you praying for a miracle?"

"No, they told me this is it. They wanted to amputate my other arm, but I said I would rather keep it so people won't have to help me so much."

Upon hearing this shocking death verdict, I anointed Jacob with the holy oils, the sacrament of healing. Happily, Jacob said, "Father, I'm going to have a surprise for you!"

It was a surprise the next day when Jacob came to receive Holy Communion, hobbling, but without his cane, and smiling.

When Jacob could no longer come to church, I brought him Communion—not the Host, only the consecrated wine, the precious blood, because he could no longer swallow.

Jacob taught me as much about medical science as he did about bravery and spiritual strength. He was given a gadget with which he could administer morphine to himself as needed. He told me, "Father, there is no pain in your lungs with cancer, because there are no nerves there. The terrible pain is when the tumor in my back presses against my ribs."

What was the secret of Jacob's strength? I asked him, "Jacob, what advice would you give others?"

"Father," he replied, "tell them never to lose faith."

The church was full for the funeral of this valiant young man. Doctors and nurses, inspired by Jacob's heroic faith, came to bid him farewell. He had even touched the hearts of some of the homeboys from his neighborhood.

Many of our people, like Jacob, find strength in their faith. I've seen many tears flow before the painting of Our Lady of Guadalupe, a mother who understands suffering. The symbols of our faith have a tremendous power.

It still makes me feel uncomfortable to tell the following story, especially after so many years of involvement in Latino culture. An old man came to the sacristy after Mass and asked for a gallon of holy water.

"No," I said. "I will get you a little bottle of holy water. You don't need a gallon." As he left, I could see that he was crushed. Father Ricardo Himes-Madero, our visitor from Mexico, enlightened me. "That was a terrible mistake! You don't understand what a powerful effect that holy water has on people who believe. His wife was dying, and he probably wanted to bathe her with holy water."

My parishioner had probably observed healing with holy water in the past. I felt terrible and hoped that he could find some *good* priest to give him a gallon of healing.

Magic and Medicine

Angel Ponce

*W*hen it comes to Latin America, both Americans and Europeans try to put together a whole continent under one single idea. This is wrong and, in many ways, completely absurd. The notion of Latin American homogeneity does not reflect the infinite ethnic and cultural variations that exist south of the Rio Grande. Argentina, Uruguay, and Chile still basically retain the ethnic and cultural traditions European settlers brought with them. In Peru, Bolivia, Ecuador, and Paraguay, an Indo-Spanish society developed from an indigenous population that still preserves the ancestral medico-religious practices inherited from the Incan and Guarani empires. Brazil, the South American giant, the only Latin American country where Portuguese is spoken, has multiple interactive ethnocultural roots. European, American Indian, and African traditions are all brilliantly manifested in her art, music, and people.

In Central America—Mexico, Guatemala, Salvador— European interlopers destroyed the Aztec and Mayan empires and in their place imposed new sociocultural patterns on a population in many ways similar to the ones found by Cortés and Pizarro during the conquest.

Described by many writers as the imperial frontier, the Caribbean exhibits numerous European influences. Spain, England, France, Holland, Portugal, and Denmark all used the Caribbean as a battleground, and each one of them left ethnic and cultural patterns on the many countries that ring this great American sea. African slaves were brought to work the plantations, taking the place of the Indian, who was rapidly exterminated or pushed deep into the South American continent by the European conquerors. Chinese and Hindus were brought as administrators and laborers to the British possessions. Many languages (English, French, Dutch, and Hindi) and many dialects (Papiamento, Taki-taki [Sranan], Garifuna) are spoken every day in this rich region in which history has created a unique syncretism of character, form, and expression. In the Caribbean, the complex ethnic and sociocultural influences take unsuspected paths, creating a giant web of puzzles and passions in which it is often impossible for a stranger to differentiate the real from the unreal. The whirlpool of colors, sounds, and textures of this magical and voluptuous universe are reflected in the works of the South American writer Gabriel García Márquez, perhaps the best-known proponent of magic realism in literature today.

I was born in the center of this complex world, in the cosmopolitan port city of San Pedro de Mecoria, Dominican Republic, in the heart of the Caribbean sugar region. My friends and their families socialized in English, French, Arab, Greek, Italian, Dutch, Chinese, Japanese, Papiamento, German, Danish, Hindi, Tagalog…the many languages and customs that melted in the Caribbean pot.

My father was a doctor, one who considered medicine as much of an art as a science. I watched him console and cure patients as varied as the foliage of our island. There was the Haitian worker, a direct descendant of a Nigerian violently uprooted centuries ago and brought chained to America; the Japanese naval officer who found his island paradise at the conclusion of World War II; the Chinese who fled communism only to encounter many who idealized the system and could not understand why he hated it; the German veteran of World War I trenches who swore never to fight again, only to find himself twenty years later a prisoner of war in Nebraska; the Spanish Republican fleeing from Franco, who finished his days in the dungeons of Trujillo; the British banker, a tall, phlegmatic, Oxford-educated Londoner, who loved whiskey and reading; the Lebanese with an almost religious sense of work and savings unknown on the islands of continual plenty; the Trinidad-born Hindu, socialist to the bone, who blamed the British for all the illnesses known to mankind from the dawn of time.

Albert Camus said that "culture is the cry of man confronting his future." In the Caribbean melting pot of the Americas, the cry is strident.

This ethnocultural syncretism of the Caribbean is present in the concept of illness, too. Reaction to disease is based on psychocultural characteristics that in the Caribbean are as varied and exuberant as nature. And of all the illnesses that afflict man, cancer is the most devastating; cancer, with its agonizing pain and its toxic treatments as traumatic as the disease itself. How have my patients dealt with the scourge of cancer? Let me introduce you to a few of them.

Evelyn, forty-one, is Dominican, Catholic, the mother of two sons. At age thirty-four, traces of cancer had been found in the peritoneum after a total hysterectomy. At the beginning, Evelyn did not want anybody to explain anything about her illness. She refused to know about her prognosis and was afraid only of the side effects of her treatment. Her husband, faced with the character of her illness and the dark prognosis, became depressed and abandoned her, leaving her alone in a strange country with two sons, eleven and six years old. After the initial shock, she decided that for the well-being of her sons, she had to survive. Something or somebody was going to help her. She went back to her gynecologist, who foresaw only catastrophic results. She refused to accept them. She discovered that a new medication, Taxol, has been effective against ovarian cancer.

The medication is still under investigation, and only a few medical centers are trying it. Evelyn discussed this with her doctor, who, after a lot of pressure, contacted the University of California at San Diego and succeeded in having her accepted for experimental treatment with Taxol. An excellent initial response was not completely confirmed in the second exploratory laparotomy. More chemotherapy, with normalization of the tumor markers, followed. Meanwhile, Evelyn had decided to enjoy life fully, wanting her sons to remember her as a loving mother, vigorous and active, always there when they needed her. She demanded excellence from her sons at work and in their studies, and her dreams materialized when her older son graduated with honors and was accepted at University of California, Berkeley. He will study medicine. He will fight against the illness that his mother fights day after day.

Evelyn confronted her titanic, never-ending battle with cancer by facing the absurdity of her condition and refusing to accept it. Yet in her struggle, she emerged as a person reaching for happiness.

Salime—Dominican, Catholic, sixty-three—was diagnosed with breast cancer. Facing the recent death by cancer of a close relative, she felt that her death was imminent, and her only request was that she be told the truth every time. She followed her doctors' advice faithfully, agreeing that they were the only ones who knew the right way. The cancer diagnosis destroyed in Salime the feeling of invulnerability that informs every person and keeps them going day after day. This new awareness of human fragility made Salime realize the irrelevance of material things. When searching for answers to her many questions, Salime reaffirmed her religious beliefs, and they have guided her toward charity and volunteerism. She found distraction by painting; she felt her creations would prolong her existence by keeping her memory alive. Today, she is living the happiest moments of her life.

Santiago, forty-five, a Garifuna from Honduras, is the direct descendant of liberated slaves. He was diagnosed with Hodgkin's disease at forty and treated initially with radiation. After three years, he had a recurrence that was treated with chemotherapy. Excellent initial results were followed by rapid recurrence a few months later. Treated again with chemotherapy, without any results this time, Santiago realized that his end was near.

When a man faces an enemy he cannot control, he often blames the supernatural, whether it is divine or evil. He may take refuge in the ancestral, ethnomagical, religious elements of his culture. Santiago discussed the course and prognosis of his illness calmly with us and came to the conclusion that demonic hidden forces were making the medicine ineffective. He decided to take refuge in the hands of a witch doctor.

Ultimately, the difference between the witch and the doctor lies in the inversion of the elements that we have on hand. In medicine, the techniques and prescriptions are mainly scientific and logical, with a minimum of magic or religion. For the witch doctor, the prescriptions and techniques are mainly magical and religious, with minimum use, if any, of science or logic. This ancient form of cure, with its many ritual secrets against the supernatural and the devilish, took over Santiago's body.

Miraculously—since we do not have another word for it—it caused an unexpected remission of his illness, allowing him to live for another year. Santiago lived his time fully, until it was impossible for the old gods of the Lucumi Kpe to interrupt the negative forces any longer.

In a modern and cosmopolitan city like Los Angeles at the beginning of the twenty-first century, it seems unreal that this ancient way of healing, based mainly on the utilization of supernatural, magical, and demonic elements, still exists. With the massive migratory movements of the last thirty years, a great wave of people for whom these ancient magico-religious elements are an important part of daily life have made the city their home and, therefore, the home of their beliefs.

As doctors, we should confront the illness as a whole and try to utilize all of the available instruments to cure the patient— without destroying him in the process. In order to obtain an effective cure, we must take the whole patient into consideration, including any preconceived ethnic and cultural patterns. In the Latin American patient, these patterns are as wide and complex as Latin America itself, making generalization very difficult. But ignorance of these ethnic and cultural factors— or the mistaken understanding of them—is the most common obstacle to the treatment of Latino patients by highly trained health professionals.

Tacos Dorados No More

Kati Szamos

Though born in Budapest, Hungary, I lived in Mexico for over thirty years, so I consider myself Mexican at heart. In Mexico, I absorbed Latin culture through every pore of my being. I take pride in its richness, its beauty, its bounty, and nowhere is this richness more vibrant than at local markets. Colors, textures, flavors explode around you, creating delicacies for the eye and the palate. While savoring the wonders of the Mexican marketplace, however, I also confronted the crude reality of the nutritional deficiencies I witnessed during the twenty years I worked in different federally funded nutrition programs in both rural and urban Mexico.

Through these years, I learned how important food is in family and community life and how significant food is to both physical and emotional well-being. I learned to understand the comfort of fatty foods and the importance of a family eating together, sharing a very small piece of meat magically worked into a soup for eight people. I have shared many such meals. I remember one occasion when I was working in a community in the Sierra of Nayarit, staying with a couple who spoke the local dialect, Huichol. Maria, the woman, was about to give birth. Though we did not speak the same language, we communicated through the preparation of meals, using the only food they had: tortillas, chilies, beans, and coffee. I helped her with the *nixtamal* (tortilla dough) and the making of tortillas. They shared all they had with me. Years later, I saw them again, in Tepic. Though they had moved to the city, their diet remained the same—with the addition of white bread and pasta soups.

While working in urban communities, I sat around many busy tables, munching on a variety of sweet breads, tamales (ground meat and chilies wrapped in cornmeal dough and steamed in corn husks), and a steaming cup of hot chocolate or *champurrado* (corn flour cooked in water with chocolate and sugar). I learned of many diet idiosyncrasies, such as frying beans in lard, and saw that what these foods lacked in nutrition, they made up for by providing comfort, cultural continuity, even pride.

The stresses and strains of immigrant life don't improve the diet of Latinos living in the United States. In my clinical work here, I see patients who know full well that their health is breaking down and even suspect that the way they eat has something to do with it. They come for diet advice, whether it is to lose weight, lower their cholesterol level, lower their blood pressure, or improve any number of nutritionally related physical conditions. But changing the way we eat is no easy task. It's hard to give up *chorizo con huevo* for breakfast or a beef, bean, or cheese burrito eaten several times a week. In their countries of origin, meat, cheese, and other fatty foods are scarce, and therefore Latinos overvalue them as icons of American prosperity.

I will tell you of one typical case. Rogelio Acosta, a factory worker, visited his doctor complaining of a variety of symptoms. He was told he was overweight and had high cholesterol and high blood pressure. The doctor sent him to me for diet therapy. When we met, I found myself facing a short and stout man, balding and overweight, who had a tired expression on his face. I perceived a certain anxiety when we shook hands. I wondered whether it had to do with getting advice from a woman or just confusion about what a dietitian really does. He asked, "What is this diet thing?" I turned the question around and asked him to tell me what it meant to *him*. His response was that he thought I was going to put him on a diet that would restrain him from eating what he liked. His enlightening answer paved the road to our success; I knew then and there that I was not going to put him on a diet and that restraint had to come in the most natural way.

I began my treatment by asking Mr. Acosta about his family and if he remembered what he had eaten as a child. He related many stories, focusing on early childhood memories of Guanajuato. The boys got together in the fields and ate corn, pumpkin seeds, and the fruit of the *mezquite* tree. Their adventures included forays into the hills for many edible fruits.

But when he was twelve, Mr. Acosta and his family moved to a larger town. His diet started to change. He still ate tortillas and *frijoles* daily, though in very little time he preferred white bread, such as *bolillos* and sweet breads bought at the *panadería*. The family was poor, yet the father found the means to feed all seven children. He told me how they would wait at the table while his mother served each of the seven children a plate of frijoles, sometimes a little meat, at times an egg, then set the bread and tortillas in the middle of the table. He had to get to the table fast so his portion would not be eaten by one of his siblings. Fruit was expensive, but he did remember eating bananas and occasionally oranges.

At seventeen, Mr. Acosta moved to the United States. As an illegal immigrant, his salary was meager during his first years here. His diet basically consisted of fast food; he rarely ate fresh vegetables and fruits. At twenty-three, he met his future wife, who is from El Salvador. Her background and preferences were similar to her husband's, and her meals still consisted primarily of tortillas, rice, frijoles, chilies, and meat. Their three children liked pizza, chips, high-sugar cereals, burgers, sodas, and chocolate. Not surprisingly, the entire family was overweight.

With this history, I knew that Mr. Acosta's dietary changes had to be gradual, that his wife had to be involved in the process, and that we needed to create a new understanding about what to eat and how to prepare foods. During our first session, we discussed what goals he wanted to achieve. After answering the nutrition questionnaires, we agreed that he would ask his wife to attend the next session as well. The three of us worked together for several months. They both learned what nutrition means, and we set step-by-step dietary goals.

As part of the process, I visited the family home to assist the wife, Maura, in the preparation of healthful foods. At the beginning, Maura knew how to boil and fry vegetables but did not think they would be palatable in any other way. I showed her many recipes and she chose the ones she wanted to try. On these visits, we prepared grilled *nopales* (cactus), vegetable soups, healthy pizzas. She discovered the magic of salads. We baked tortilla chips and prepared enchiladas without frying the tortillas. Over onions, tomatoes, lentils, garbanzos, and other simple and nutritious foods, we explored her beliefs about health, weight, and food. Often I ate at their table and talked to their children about my son, José, who was "forced" to grow up with a dietitian. I helped them create a "sweet box" to hold all their goodies, like chocolate, candy, and chips, from which they could take a piece once a day.

For six months, one of Mr. Acosta's assignments was to keep a food diary, a record of everything he ate, both at home and outside the home. We evaluated the diary together by making charts and breaking his food choices down into fats, sugars, protein, starches, fruits, and vegetables. He learned about food combinations, dietary guidelines for healthful eating, and how to cut out and substitute those food items that were working against his health. I could tell that he was quite excited by the knowledge he was acquiring. As he started losing weight, he told me he was passing on dietary tips to his factory coworkers.

I asked Maura to call me on a regular basis so we could talk about recipes, about the children, or about any other issue on her mind. At first I thought that she was defensive, that her mind was not open to change. I was quite wrong. She was eager for knowledge yet scared she would not live up to the "standard" of a professional dietitian. She came to realize that changing the family's eating habits was an adventure that could be fun when everyone at home was involved. She discovered that eating healthfully was actually inexpensive and effective.

Mr. Acosta successfully adjusted to new ways of eating and reached his dietary goals. This was no simple task, for contemporary nutritional knowledge has not penetrated significantly in the Latino community. Not only is there a language barrier, there are also cultural biases that need to be addressed. The challenge for us, the health professionals, is to help Latinos achieve nutritional adequacy while maintaining the essence of Latino cuisine, with its exquisite flavors, textures, and ingredients. Latinos will be Latinos, whether it's *tacos dorados*—fried tacos—or *tacos dorados* no more.

Body and Soul

Curanderismo

Roberto Chiprut

*L*atinos feel that in order to obtain absolute healing, there has to be a balance between the emotions (which is their fantasy) and the body (which is their reality). *Curanderos*, traditional healers, are essential in preserving this psychological balance in Latino culture.

Curanderos do not separate physical from psychological problems, as Western medicine is accustomed to doing. Curanderos treat the whole person with techniques that combine medical remedies with spiritual, even religious, solutions. Faith is the ultimate healing modality, available when nothing else works. Although Western medicine has taken root in the majority of Latino communities, both in Latin America and here in the United States, it will never completely eradicate the folk-healing curandero and the solace of spiritual healing, often attained through magic.

Latino patients may seek the help of the curandero for strictly physical ailments, but many visits to the curandero are of an emotional or cultural nature: unhappiness with Western medicine, confidence in what the curandero offers, and learned attitudes about health, which have a strong influence on the patient's decision making.

In general, many Latinos feel that the curandero has supernatural powers, as well as a vast medical expertise. Ironically, this creates ambivalence, for most believe that curanderos can either heal or harm, depending on their use of "good" or "evil" powers. It can be difficult to distinguish between curanderos who heal and those who practice only "black magic."

In spite of the stunning advances of modern medicine, the curandero still holds enormous influence in Latino culture. Particularly in the case of cancer and other chronic diseases for which there is no clear medical solution, it is not uncommon for patients to appeal to the curandero. Perhaps it is something about the hands-on nature of *curanderismo*—the way it involves the patient, the patient's family, and the patient's world—that seems to soothe. The mere act of preparing or administering some kind of herbal home remedy provides a strong emotional support, whether done by the patient or a family member. Preparing herbs, performing rituals, and giving massages demonstrate affection, care, and empowerment. This is what healing is all about. The patient's recovery is promoted by the improvement of psychological outlook—regardless of how effective the treatment was. This holistic approach to healing, so typical of folk medicine, has recently been taken up by Western health care practitioners who view good health as a system in which the physical and the emotional work together and sustain each other.

As long as Western medical practitioners ignore the cultural values of the Latino patient, the curandero will remain an integral part of Latino medical behavior. But as we attempt to understand the importance of curanderismo—and other folk medical systems—to the total health of our patients, and as we, too, attempt to provide our patients with spiritual sustenance, both our patients and the Western medical establishment will benefit. Only when a true partnership exists between the curandero and the Western practitioner will we achieve a balance between reality and fantasy in the Latino patient.

Discovering Curanderismo

Cristina Orcí Fernández

I have sprained my ankle three times in my life, and I received three very different kinds of treatments for it. The trials and tribulations of this poor ankle can provide some insight into the comparative methods of Western medicine and the *curandero* of Latino culture. The first time I sprained my ankle, I simply tripped on a crack outside my parents' house in Los Angeles. But my ankle quickly swelled to three times its normal size and I was in so much pain that I asked to be taken to the emergency room. There, after a four-hour wait, I was treated by an American MD who ordered X-rays, prescribed anti-inflammatories, painkillers, and rest, and handed me a brand new pair of crutches, which I used for two weeks. She was very nice. She never touched my ankle.

The second time I sprained my ankle, I was in rural southern Mexico, teaching bank skills to the managers of an 870-member weavers' cooperative at their store in San Cristóbal de las Casas.

Instead of visiting a physician this time, a friend took me to
see a local *huesero*, or bonesetter. Don Lupe sat in a chair
opposite me, took my affected ankle in his hands, and, after a
short invocation of the saints, went to the task. His technique
involved hands-on manipulation of the sprain (*luxación*) using
a combination of pressure, traction, and resistance to realign
my tendons and muscles and thus restore movement and function. His push-and-pull therapy seemed to go on forever, and
it was incredibly painful. Don Lupe wasn't as personable as
that American MD had been, and he certainly caused me a lot
more pain in the short term. But I'd gone in his door limping
and I left walking.

I was still in Mexico the third (and last) time I sprained my
ankle. This time I visited another huesero, Don Pancho, famous
for a technique called *la ventosa*, which he had learned from
his father-in-law. He tucked a piece of cotton into a ball of wax
placed in a brandy snifter. He lit the cotton with a match, then
placed the mouth of the snifter right above my lateral malleolus.
When the flame went out, a vacuum was created. Don Pancho
then moved the glass up and down the side of my leg, and the
vacuum literally lifted my muscles and tendons and returned
them to their rightful places. The inflammation went down
almost immediately.

My experience with curanderos and their ways of healing,
however, began well before I visited Don Lupe in Chiapas in
1992. My grandmother Jesusita, a practicing herbalist, used to
give me foul-tasting but oddly comforting remedies when I was
ill. From her, I learned the value of the herb-based, ritualistic
remedies so important to healing in the Latino community. I
also began to understand how these remedies could comple-
ment the treatment available at the doctor's office. I became
a student of herbs while I was in Mexico working with the
weaving cooperative. During my time in San Cristóbal de las

Casas, I had the opportunity to study the connections between curanderismo and Western medicine in a very intimate way.

An understanding of curanderismo is a valuable tool for practitioners who want to help Latino patients manage health, prevent disease, and engage healing responses more effectively. Curanderismo is not a single approach or technique. Rather, it is a dynamic system with its own theory of the origins of disease and a diverse array of healing modalities offered by a variety of specialists. Together, these disciplines address the whole human being at the physical, emotional, and spiritual levels.

Transmitted by word of mouth, curanderismo is a remedy-based system in which faith, prayer (or visualization), traditional wisdom, observation, and the scientific method combine to effect healing. The oral pharmacopoeia of curanderismo—the collective knowledge of the culture—is constantly being shared, re-created, and augmented. Curanderismo, in a similar way, is constantly transforming itself, embracing new tools and healing modalities that have proven effective through time and worthy of faith. In this way, curanderismo is not a substitute for Western medicine, but actually embraces it as one of its modalities.

But I had little formal understanding of the world of curanderismo when I arrived in Mexico. The project that initially brought me to Chiapas aimed to help establish economic self-sufficiency among the women of the area. My immersion in the world of traditional healing came as a result of that work, an involvement I would not have predicted when I arrived. As women brought textiles from their remote communities to the cooperative store in San Cristóbal, I noticed that many of them were ill and needed medical attention. I discussed what I was seeing with one of the Indian store managers, Micaela Hernández, and we decided to expand our services to help them. Suddenly, we became health promoters. We sought out gynecologists and general practitioners charging reduced fees, nonprofit organizations delivering both traditional medicine and Western health services, foot reflexologists, and Indian acupuncturists. We also forged alliances with the nursing staffs at government clinics and hospitals.

Between 1992 and 1994, we helped many women and families gain access to health services, including reproductive and prenatal care. In 1995, the MacArthur Foundation awarded our nonprofit organization, K'inal Antzetik (Women's Earth), a generous grant to run a two-year health promoter training program. During that time, thanks to the vision and the hard work of Blanca Espinosa, RN; we also formalized a relationship between K'inal health promoters and the nursing staff and social workers at the Hospital de Campo in San Cristóbal.

While it was certainly my goal to demystify Western medicine for the Indian women, as a nonspecialist I could understand the confusion and frustration that visits to the physician occasioned. Our family doctor prescribed antibiotics for everything—diarrhea, colds, coughs, sinus infections, you name it. But we got sick often enough in Chiapas—six or seven times a year—that reliance on them would soon build up resistance. And a close reading of the box for chloramphenicol, the only medicine available for typhoid fever (a common ailment in Chiapas) revealed that it can cause aplastic anemia! It all seemed very dangerous to me. So when the health promoters visited the Organization of Traditional Indian Doctors of Chiapas (OMIECh), I was introduced to a vast supply of herbal remedies good for everything from expelling intestinal worms to recovering lost souls. We all stocked up on a few basic herbs and set to the task of healing ourselves and our families. I became the herbalist and health advocate in my household, as did the health promoters in their own communities.

I still relied on the doctor for the diagnosis, but I began listening closely to old wives' tales for the remedies. Cornsilk and parsley for ten days for urinary tract infections. *Wash te vomol* for typhoid fever for twenty days. Dandelion for gastritis. *Tizana betel* for the nerves. Shredded raw potato leaches out the poison of a dog bite. Belladonna can kill; stay away. Put cut aloe vera fronds on burns or around the neck for tonsillitis. Cayenne pepper stanches the flow of blood immediately from deep knife cuts. Never eat when you're angry. Pass an egg all over a fussy baby's body, front and back. Wear a red sash under your clothes to ward off the evil eye. I was also astonished to learn that Indian shepherd women observe what their sheep eat when they have diarrhea or fever and use the same herbs when it is time to cure themselves.

In my quest for healers, I met bonesetters and midwives, paramedics and health promoters, German acupuncturists and Indian seers, old women and urban conjurers. I also met a lot of MDs who had found that integrating the techniques and tools of curanderismo made them more effective in establishing rapport with and healing their patients. MDs who work in remote locations, whether they're fulfilling community service requirements or their mission in life, are faced with serious obstacles. The communities they serve often have few resources and a very poor health infrastructure, if there is one at all. The practice of medicine based strictly on pharmaceuticals is virtually impossible. In Chiapas before 1994, most rural community clinics couldn't even be counted on to have the most basic first-aid materials, like alcohol and gauze.

Claudia Meza, MD, who works with the COLEM Women's Collective in San Cristóbal, says that her solid knowledge of local herbs and healing modalities is critical to her work. She builds rapport readily with her patients, Indian and non-Indian alike, because she is familiar with their healing traditions and works them into her treatment plans. She also asks about other practitioners they've visited and what their diagnoses were. She prescribes soothing herbs for the nerves, bitter herbs for gastritis, and a pharmaceutical drug, Zentel, to expel worms. She also recommends that her patients go to the mystic herbalist for a *limpia*, or cleansing, to clear negative energy.

"Since most of our patients are very poor," says Dr. Meza, "we can't rely on pharmaceutical medicine alone. I am limited to the samples and donations that our organization gets. Besides, some of my patients don't have faith in pharmaceuticals and prefer to use natural means to cure themselves." But she also agrees that pharmaceuticals are increasingly accepted in the local community, even deified to an extent. More and more young people are saying that herbs don't work and professing their faith in antibiotics. Still, Dr. Meza prefers to use herbal and nutritional cures because she knows that malnutrition, common in her patients, opens the way for other diseases.

The highlands of Chiapas provide a fascinating microcosm in which the healing disciplines that make up curanderismo are interwoven in a rich tapestry. In the curanderismo model, health is not simply the absence of disease in a person, but a state of emotional, physical, and spiritual balance. When that balance is upset, disease follows. Illnesses fall into three categories:

- Physical diseases are caused by parasites (producing diarrhea, nausea, and constipation), saturation from overeating (*empacho*), or bad air (*aire*). Bad air can lead to sprains, dislocations, rheumatism, and joint pain.
- Emotional diseases are a response to strong reactions in the body, such as a sudden fright (*susto*), an angry outburst (*coraje* or *bilis*), or excess worry (*nervios*), or strong feelings of envy (*envidia*) or selfishness (*egoismo*).
- Diseases in the spiritual realm can come as punishment for bad deeds, unresolved traumas from this life or previous lives, or spells. Conditions like insomnia, nightmares, epilepsy (*ataques*), and shock (*atarantamiento*) are sometimes

attributed to accumulated negative energy or spells cast by others. Diseases can also be sent by God to punish either individuals or entire communities that have broken the rules.

These ailments can be treated by any number of therapies. Relatives and friends are certain to recommend their favorite modalities and practitioners. Ultimately, however, patients choose their practitioners based on what their faith tells them.

These are some of the curanderos I met during my years in Chiapas:

Yerberas (Herbalists)

Mothers are the foremost herbalists and curanderas. Old wives and their tales are their teachers, the home is their laboratory, and the oral pharmacopoeia is their textbook. They administer herbs to manage the health and disease of their children as a matter of course. They are also the health promoters in their families: they monitor their sick and take them to the appropriate practitioners.

Professional yerberas base their practices on herbs, rituals, and prayers for protection and healing. They concoct, prescribe, and administer teas, broths, and tinctures and apply mud packs and herbal poultices and liniments. They generally treat diseases with physical and emotional causes.

Most yerberas begin their careers healing members of their immediate family and their animals. As their skill grows, they begin offering their talents to their extended family and, later, their neighborhood. Some yerberas acquire such fame that people travel great distances to be healed by them.

Yerberas conduct *limpias*, or cleansings, in which they clear negative energy by slapping bouquets of astringent herbs over the patient's body. They also use an egg to detect the presence of a curse, or the evil eye, on a patient. The yerbera passes the egg lightly over the patient's body while asking the saints to intercede. The egg is said to extract the negative energy in the body. When they break the egg open in a clear glass filled with water, the source of the malaise is often clarified: the shape of an eye present in the yolk or the white indicates the evil eye, whereas a black spot might indicate stagnant energy due to someone's envy of or jealousy toward the patient. Some herbalists also sprinkle holy water (blessed by a priest) in homes and new vehicles as a measure of protection. MDs like Dr. Claudia Meza prescribe similar kinds of rituals for patients with chronic ailments or depression.

True to the assertion that curanderismo is a remedy-based system, many herbalists in Chiapas are increasingly integrating pharmaceuticals, specifically antibiotics and painkillers, into the oral pharmacopoeia and prescribing them to patients.

Iloles/Videntes/Curanderas (Conjurers/Seers/ Shamans/Healers)

Iloles are traditional Indian doctors and personal spiritual guides. They treat ailments that originate in the spirit and have physical manifestations. They can also help patients to let go of strong emotional states, such as envy and jealousy, that cause disease in the body. They diagnose largely through pulse, interviews, and the interpretation of the patient's dreams. Some practitioners in Chiapas also consult an ancient Mayan oracle called simply "the box."

The tools of the *ilol* are copal incense, meditation, and prayer, fragrant herbs and flowers, and the complicity of the person to be healed. Patients are active participants in the conjurer's ritual. They lie close to altars filled with sacred herbs while the seer visits the church and the sanctuaries in the caves and mountaintops. Then patients must buy the candles of many colors that will be arranged on the church floor at the time of the healing.

But the work of the iloles is not limited strictly to the spiritual plane. In the 1980s, a group of iloles created OMIECh under the umbrella of the National Indian Institute (INI, Instituto Nacional Indigenista). Their goal was to provide a mechanism whereby the oral tradition could be systematically recorded, scientifically tested, and formally shared with doctors, health organizations, and individuals wanting to learn the science of the ancestors. OMIECh became independent in the early 1990s and has since conducted important pharmacological studies of herbs traditionally used to treat common infectious diseases. They have extensive photographic records of local plants and flowers and exhaustive records of their chemical components.

Hueseros (Bonesetters)

Hueseros are the most earth-based practitioners. They are part chiropractor, part physical therapist, and even part psychologist. They set broken bones and realign sprained or dislocated joints using pressure, traction, and resistance. They treat inflammation, bone pain, and broken spirits. A huesero practices the techniques learned as an apprentice. While some practitioners were clearly born into the practice, others simply learned the skill from a close relative or family friend.

Some hueseros can even tell by pulsation whether a fracture, sprain, or inflammation requires cold herbs or heating herbs to counteract it. They work with lotions or camphor-based ointments, and some dispense herbal remedies as well. For setting bones, they use rolled newspapers, boards, popsicle sticks, and whatever other tools are available. After childbirth, women visit a huesero to "close" the pelvis.

Parteras (Midwives)

Like the ilol, the midwife dreams about her patient and how to care for her. The midwife is the gatekeeper between the spiritual and the physical worlds. She uses her hands to position the baby for birth. She welcomes the child into this world, then bathes the new mother in sacred herbs gathered at sunrise. For forty days, the woman is cared for by mother, sisters, neighbors.

But midwives might be becoming a thing of the past. Rosa González, a midwife, weaver, and mother of six living in the remote mountain enclave of Jolxic, explains one of the reasons:

"I am a midwife by training, but I don't practice anymore. In my life, I have helped many women with the births of their children. But now families are blaming midwives if the women or the babies die during labor. Right now there are two midwives in jail because the women died. But sometimes there is nothing they can do to save them."

In addition, many women have discovered that giving birth in hospitals is a viable alternative. And many women make the journey to San Cristóbal to give birth at a clinic if there isn't a midwife in their community.

At the same time, however, other women are organizing to preserve and promote their craft. The traditional midwives of OMIECh have been researching the oral history, techniques, and herbs of midwifery. With other health-oriented nonprofit organizations, they published a book of full-color photographs of local herbs used before, during, and after labor.

Espiritistas (Channelers)

Channelers attend, almost exclusively, to ailments of the spirit: souls separated from their bodies and past life trauma.

After many journeys to Mexico City to visit neurologists and psychiatrists and suffering many disagreeable tests, Laura was finally diagnosed at age nineteen with paranoid schizophrenia. But her bizarre and unpredictable behavior continued, despite the pharmaceutical medicine she was taking. As a last resort, her family decided to take her to the Centro Espiritista in Tuxtla, the capital of Chiapas.

At the center, patients stay from one day to one week. Channelers conduct diagnostic rituals involving tarot cards, wax, or coffee grounds. They conduct *limpias* with bouquets of herbs and an egg. They recite chanted prayers to the saints and prescribe rituals that patients are to follow at home. "Every day after my sister came home, we had to sprinkle salt in the corners of her room, then mop it with a brew of special herbs and other things I can't talk about," said Laura's sister, Mayra.

Espiritistas channel the patient's guides and spirits for information about the source of their illness. Espiritistas can know, then, whether or not the disease is caused by a spell—and who cast it. Espiritistas fall into two camps: those who tell their patients who cast the spell and those who do not, arguing that it only jeopardizes their patient's healing process.

Laura's practitioners would not tell her who cast the spell, but they confirmed that it was indeed the source of her illness. She stayed at the center for a week, experienced a course of treatment, and, when she returned home, felt (and behaved) "like before." Her condition improved and during the following year she was able to finish high school. She visited the center weekly for a few months. But one day, she began hearing voices again. She had a relapse and was kept at home for some time. With the help of the channelers, Laura has once again been able to control her illness, though her future is uncertain.

Sobadoras (Massage Therapists)

Sobadoras are the massage therapists of the community. All the sobadoras I've ever met are little old ladies with a special gift. They do their household chores all day, but they will always take a moment to treat the children brought to them by worried mothers. Sobadoras use massage to treat *empacho* (saturation from overeating), constipation, and diarrhea. They dab alcohol on the feet to bring down fever. Some give full body massages and others are skilled in visceral manipulation. They may concoct and administer brews and work with lotions, oils, and alcohol. Many sobadoras are also midwives or hueseras.

Health Promoters

Health promoters are an important part of the health care system in the highlands of Chiapas, but they are not limited to that area. The health promoter model is used all over Mexico and in impoverished nations all over the world as a way of giving communities tools, resources, and a referral system to manage health and disease with confidence.

The first Indian health promoters were trained in the early 1960s by INI to take Western medicine to people in remote rural communities, but they were not immediately accepted. In the 1970s, these first health promoters were also pioneers in the field of parallel medicine, which began exploring the ways in which traditional Indian medicine and Western medicine intersected in the panorama of health services in the region.

Indian health promoters became the bridge between traditional Indian medicine and Western medicine, between rural communities and health services in urban centers. Government health institutions and nascent health-oriented nonprofit groups began training health promoters to provide the first level of service in their communities and to refer people to the nearest clinic if their skills were insufficient or the condition too advanced. The existence of health promoters helped make up for the deficiencies in the health infrastructure that barely existed in Indian communities. Health promoters also offered people a measure of power in knowing about and choosing their options for healing.

I know of one nurse/health promoter who single-handedly provided health services to hundreds of families that had no access to a clinic. Antonio Santiz had an economically strapped client base and neither government support nor organizational affiliation. But he had a skill, and his people were sick. He also had connections with doctors and clinics for people willing to leave their homes. And he had plenty of faith that God would continue to provide. People would pay him what they could: a chicken, a dozen eggs, a sack of beans. He found himself working eighteen-hour days and scratching out prescriptions on paper napkins he acquired at restaurants.

After working to improve access to health services for women and children for two years, K'inal Antzetik, together with several members of the weavers' cooperative, developed a health promoter training program specifically for women. Most promoters in the communities, if there were any, were men. And, as we learned, women were willing to discuss issues of health, and particularly reproductive health, only with women. They were much more willing to seek health services when provided with information and accompaniment.

Between 1995 and 1997, thirty-five women and five men from eleven communities participated in K'inal Antzetik's health promoter training program. The curriculum was created and taught by Blanca Espinosa, who insists that it is not enough to tell people to wash their hands or to boil their water: "They have to see what's happening. In one of our first experiments, we collected dirty water and looked at it through the microscope. Once the women saw living organisms, it didn't take them long to realize why it's important to boil the water. And why it's important to wash your hands."

In the training program, health promoters learned to navigate the complex system of health services and to provide intervention and referrals in high-risk pregnancies and unforeseen emergencies. They studied anatomy, first aid, and CPR and learned how to administer injections and IVs. They gathered the women in their communities and gave talks about health-related subjects previously chosen by the group. Blanca integrated foot reflexology, acupuncture, and relaxation techniques into the curriculum. She also stressed women's reproductive health and the importance of women understanding their own bodies.

Most health promoters were already herbalists to varying degrees and so incorporated this expertise into the range of services they could provide for their community members. They were also able to access the services provided by OMIECh, the organization of traditional doctors. Also, thanks to Blanca, the relationship between K'inal health promoters and the Hospital de Campo in San Cristóbal was formalized in 1995. Blanca continues to be the bridge between the health promoters and the clinics. She is constantly demystifying Western medical practice for Indian patients and traditional Indian medicine for the medical doctors who serve them.

Though the project is over, the health promoters continue to provide services in their communities and participate in more specialized training. Many Indian men and women in Chiapas have even learned acupuncture from a committed visitor. Every day, health promoters become better referral sources; since their circles usually include an eclectic mix of health practitioners, they are familiar with a wide range of healing modalities available for their patients.

Perhaps the story told to me by Yolanda Castro, a founder of K'inal Antzetik, best illustrates how health care works in the rural regions of Mexico. In this story, both practitioners of curanderismo and of Western medicine intersect in the life of one woman.

In a small, dark hut with a packed dirt floor, a shadowy Petrona lay sleeping in the bed, white as a clean sheet and with an IV in her arm. The silence was so total that each drop of fluid could be heard. It was nightfall, and she was still hemorrhaging after a miscarriage that morning. The midwife explained that Petrona had miscarried because she'd made a *coraje*—someone had made her very angry that morning.

An altar in the corner showed that the ilol had already been there. Incense burned steadily, and the flickering candles on the floor cast ghostly shapes on the whitewashed walls. The silence was broken now and then by the whispered greetings of a woman shaking hands with all fifteen women sitting in chairs along the perimeter of the room. As she took her place, another would rise and leave.

Again the silence was broken, this time by several women singing a prayer asking for the blood to stop. Petrona knew they were there and was thankful, but could not open her eyes. Women came bearing buckets of chicken soup, others a dozen eggs, and still others sacks of corn for Petrona and her family.

Soon Antonio, the lone community health promoter in the region, arrived with medicine he had found through a nonprofit organization in San Cristóbal, an hour away by bus. Petrona was losing blood quickly and this medicine was certainly the last hope. As night wore on, the women continued to sit quietly beside Petrona, lighting candles for her and watching over her, reminding her wandering soul that her place was among them.

The next day, Dr. Barbara Cadenas visited Petrona to make sure the medicine was helping her improve. She had already arranged emergency transportation to the regional hospital in the capital, four hours away, in case Petrona's condition had worsened during the night. Fortunately, it had not, so she was able to stay at home.

The women never left her side. When Petrona stood up five days later to go to San Cristóbal for an ultrasound and to pray at seven churches with her ilol, they saw her off.

Curanderismo as a system is the expression of a culture desiring to find balance in an unpredictable and often unkind world. When we see curanderismo as a system of healing modalities and practitioners, it's clear that Western medicine fits neatly into the scheme. Latinos are willing to integrate new modalities and practitioners into their network of health care providers. They do, however, have to become familiar with the process and feel comfortable in the environment in which it unfolds. Most important, they have to have faith in the practitioner. Herein lies the task of the health care provider: to make Western medicine accessible, comprehensible, and worthy of faith for Latino patients.

Many Indian women I met in Chiapas wouldn't set foot in a clinic because "no one comes out of there alive." However, once they entered and met the secretary, the dentist, the ob-gyn, the social workers, and the nurses, their fear was replaced by curiosity. Finally, they were comfortable enough to ask questions and to consider that perhaps those who didn't come out alive had postponed coming until it really was too late.

Many times, Latinos are too shy to ask questions lest they seem to be questioning the doctor's authority. But as Western doctors begin to ask questions themselves, the barriers that exist between the culture of their Latino patients and the technological world of the MD will begin to come down. Latinos will more comfortably integrate Western medicine and doctors into their constellation of healing modalities and healers. And Western doctors will become much more knowledgeable about healing Latinos and will take their place as respected and trusted healers in the community.

Si Dios Nos Da Licencia

If God Permits

Juan Villagomez

*I*n June 1996, I was diagnosed with stomach cancer. I had been endoscoped on May 28, 1996, to evaluate several months of gastrointestinal symptoms of heartburn and abdominal pain. Two days after the endoscopy, on May 30, I participated in California AIDS Ride 3, a seven-day, 525-mile cycling trek from San Francisco to Los Angeles, during which over 1,800 riders raised over $8 million for HIV and AIDS care. On the evening of June 8, while I celebrated the conclusion of the ride, my friend Dr. Martha Hierro, who had done my endoscopy, arrived at my home with a bottle of champagne. She then shared the final pathology report of my stomach biopsy, which showed cells of adenocarcinoma.

After extensive evaluation over the next two weeks, I was estimated to have a 20 percent chance of surviving five years. I underwent four months of chemotherapy and had a total gastrectomy in August 1996. I was unable to practice medicine for over nine months. I returned to practice part-time in February 1997. From June 1 to June 7, 1997, I participated in California AIDS Ride 4 from San Francisco to Los Angeles. My four brothers and I rode 585 miles with 2,400 cyclists and helped raise $9.4 million for HIV and AIDS care. I did the ride as a cancer survivor.

Cancer has changed my life. I have lived through the fears, despair, and depression of fighting a potentially terminal illness. During the months of treatment, I struggled with feelings of despair and depression. I had recurrent intrusive thoughts, images, and dreams of dying. I cried for my children. I feared that I would leave them orphaned at such a young age. My son, Roberto, was three years old, and my daughter, Gabriela, was sixteen months when I was diagnosed.

Fortunately, I received tremendous love, support, and prayers from my family, friends, patients, church, and colleagues, which gave me courage, hope, and strength. When I underwent my first year's complete evaluation, it showed no recurrence of cancer. I continue to pray and receive blessings from others.

Having been a patient for nine months, I found myself treating, talking to, and touching my patients much differently than I had before. I was more in tune with healing and prayer, especially in treating my patients with major medical problems: cancer, AIDS, heart failure, diabetes, and other illnesses.

I feel empathy with my patients. Physically, I have felt the nausea of chemotherapy, the pain of surgery, the hurt of inserting a urinary catheter, the nasal and throat pain of having a nasogastric tube, the excruciating pain of bowel obstructions and colonic spasms, the numbness of feet and hands, and tinnitus with sporadic hearing loss from the side effects of the chemotherapy. I've felt the profound weakness and nausea brought on by chemotherapy. Emotionally, I sank into the abyss of despair and depression. I have struggled with feelings of impending doom. I much better understand both the feelings and the physical symptoms and apprehensions that most patients feel. I gained an invaluable gift through my hardships and struggles.

At the same time, the positive and nurturing aspects have affected me, too. I learned to pause and pray. I learned to meditate. I received the healing touch of spiritual prayer. At times, I felt an inner warmth, hard to explain, that felt whole and healing.

Upon my return to part-time clinical practice in Santa Monica in February 1997, I focused much of my practice on the care of my elderly patients, 80 percent of whom are Latino. My patients suffer from the common ailments of the elderly, including diabetes, hypertension, congestive heart failure, chronic obstructive pulmonary disease, arthritis, depression, and cancer.

Each elderly person is a wealth of priceless life experiences. I enjoy the challenge of helping with both medical and emotional needs. I enjoy the challenge of working with family dynamics in moments of crisis. I enjoy helping families through the many stages and struggles of life, illness, dying, and death.

Mrs. Doris Marmolejo was born in Bogotá, Colombia. She immigrated to California in 1965, at thirty-five, with her husband and son, settling in Culver City in a neighborhood with other Colombians and Cubans. She worked for over twenty years at the Gillette Papermate assembly plant in Santa Monica until she retired. Her husband died in 1970 of cirrhosis.

I first met Mrs. Marmolejo on January 29, 1992. She was then sixty-one and was suffering from arthritis and hypertension. She had been experiencing several months of abdominal bloating, and physical examination revealed blood in her stool and anemia. She was referred to a gastroenterologist, who performed an upper endoscopy which revealed a fungating mass in the stomach that pathology reported as gastric adenocarcinoma.

Mrs. Marmolejo suffered from abdominal spasms, cramps and pains, weight loss, and depression. Yet during her office visits, her most endearing quality was her humor and wry spirit. She would start many visits with a joke, funny story, or even better, a dirty X-rated joke. We would laugh, and I regret not having written some of her jokes down.

On December 3, 1992, she was hospitalized for esophageal strictures and acute cholecystitis. At that time, she underwent open cholecystectomy and esophageal dilatation. Two months later, February 1993, she was hospitalized with acute pancreatitis.

For three years, from February 1993 through May 1996, Mrs. Marmolejo remained in good health. She was still bothered several times per week with abdominal discomfort and pain from reflux esophagitis. I would see her every two to three months. She would come in with a least two or three of her hilariously funny and crude *chistes* (jokes). She was well read and extremely intelligent—a warm, caring woman. She lived every day with enthusiasm and zeal. She would volunteer to help a local Latino geriatric support group through WISE (Westside Independent Services for the Elderly). She attended Catholic Mass several times per week at Saint Gerard's in Culver City.

Then, in June 1996, Dr. Hierro showed me my final biopsy report, which showed gastric adenocarcinoma. I sat in shock, reading adenocarcinoma over and over. I stayed awake with recurrent thoughts of dying and death. I kept having images of my children growing up without their father. I cried with anguish that evening as I envisioned my passing. Later, as I slept, I went from one nightmare into another with images of death and darkness. But, on the Monday morning after my AIDS ride and my diagnosis with stomach cancer, I tried to resume being a doctor.

Mrs. Marmolejo had been added to an already packed morning. I had last seen her four months prior; she had been feeling well. That morning, she had been experiencing progressively worsening shortness of breath. An X-ray showed multiple pulmonary nodules consistent with metastatic tumors. I admitted her to Saint John's Hospital for her shortness of breath and obtained pulmonary and oncologic consultations to discuss treatment options.

It was horrifically difficult not to feel my own despair and fear of death while I treated Mrs. Marmolejo. Likewise, it was difficult for me to share with her my own diagnosis of stomach cancer, but I did. Dr. Hierro was also her gastroenterologist. She and I sat in the doctor's dictation room and cried together.

During my treatment for gastric cancer, I kept in touch with Mrs. Marmolejo. I started my chemotherapy in June with two months of continuous treatment via a right subclavian port-a-catheter, which was a one-inch-diameter plastic port under my skin through which a large-bore needle infused chemotherapy, pain medication, and antinausea medication. In August 1996, I had a total gastrectomy and splenectomy requiring a nine-day hospitalization. I finished my chemotherapy at Norris University of Southern California Cancer Hospital with daily intra-abdominal chemotherapy for one week in September and a final treatment in October 1996. Both one-week cycles of chemotherapy caused extreme nausea, weakness, and a dreadful feeling of illness that twice required hospitalization at Saint John's Hospital in Santa Monica. Mrs. Marmolejo would call me there, and we would share comforting prayers and wishes.

I felt sorrow and sadness that Mrs. Marmolejo was dying, and guilt that I was healing and doing better while Mrs. Marmolejo was coming to the end of her life. It was a nightmarish experience—fighting my stomach cancer while watching Mrs. Marmolejo dying of hers. Still, she always had a kind word and a humorous joke to liven up the moment. I last saw her on December 19, 1996. She and I sat together, shared a kiss and a warm embrace, and silently said good-bye to each other. She died in a skilled nursing facility on March 12, 1997.

Recently, I have attended several wakes and funeral masses for close patients who died of prolonged illnesses. After the death of one of my patients from cancer, I couldn't stop weeping; I felt a personal loss. I kept thinking of my own possible impending death. I began to have recurrent feelings that my cancer would return; fear of recurrence is a haunting specter, constantly present.

It's been difficult being both patient and physician. I've been engulfed by feelings of empathy and sympathy, of compassion and comparison, of professional distance and personal feelings. Before my illness, it was easy to treat one patient after another, feel empathy but move on to the next patient, the next interpersonal crisis. I had sympathy for my patients, but seldom to the point of personal attachment. After returning to clinical practice after my own cancer, empathy with patients was stronger and more disturbing as I tried to be an objective physician. I felt too close to the experience of being a patient, especially having gone down the difficult road of depression, chemotherapy, surgery, and pain. From the simple discomfort of obtaining blood for laboratory analysis to the morass of overwhelming despair after the diagnosis—I know these sensations. Since my return to clinical practice, I have diagnosed twenty patients with some form of cancer, among them malignant melanoma, colon cancer, breast cancer, lymphoma, lung cancer, stomach cancer, vaginal cancer, uterine cancer, and prostate cancer. At times, it feels overwhelming.

But most of the time, I feel strong and embrace each patient I encounter with compassion and hope, trying to live each day to the fullest—*si Dios nos da licencia* (if God permits).

* * *

Dr. Juan Villagomez succumbed to cancer in October 1999, with family and friends around him, at peace, knowing he had done his best in this life.

Glossary

Abuela (dim., *Buelita*). Grandmother.

Andale. Go ahead. Lyrics to a song that praises drinking.

Barrio. A Latino neighborhood.

Bilis. Bile. May refer to anger as a personality trait. *Se le derramó la bilis* (there was a spillage of bile) reflects a state of sudden anger resulting in an illness.

Borracho. A state of inebriation; a drunk.

Canciones de mi padre. Songs that my father sang. The title of Linda Ronstadt's album of Mexican music. In Latino culture, people sing songs that may be over a century old, yet still popular.

Cariño. Tender affection.

Chicano. Commonly refers to a person born in the United States of Mexican parents or grandparents. Also refers to a Latino with an acute sense of political commitment.

Chistes. Jokes. May be used to relieve tension or distract from the reality of an occasion. In Latino culture, laughter can be paramount in the healing process.

Clínica. A small doctor's office where a wide variety of services may be provided. Patients can see their doctor without an appointment. Most Latino neighborhoods in Southern California have a *clínica*. The layout of these clinics frequently resembles that of federally funded health care clinics in Mexico.

Cumplir con su deber. To fulfill one's duty. A *dicho.* The determination to comply with this maxim can be part of the macho personality.

Curandera. Latino lay folk healer. A person with special powers who uses a wide variety of methods to heal folk illnesses.

Día de los Muertos. The Day of the Dead, celebrated on All Saints Day (Nov. 1). In Latin America, a special celebration in which altars are constructed and food offerings made to the departed souls of deceased family members, who are invited to spend time with the living.

Dichos. Sayings or folk aphorisms. Common phrases with a deep philosophical background.

Dios. God, in whose hands major medical decisions are left.

Dolor de cabeza. Headache. Could be part of any folk ailment containing a strong psychosomatic component. Folk healing methods are often employed to treat it. Latinos often use combination drugs, not available in this country, that are bought across the border or sent by family members.

Emociones. Strong emotions, which may trigger an illness.

Empacho. Condition of abdominal discomfort that can be the result of food consumption. In Latino folk medicine, *empacho* refers to food stuck in the upper abdomen. Common remedies include the use of laxatives or abdominal massage by the mother or a *sobadora.*

Envidia. Envy. Envious feelings may generate a *mal de ojo,* resulting in the development of an illness.

Espiritista. A spiritual healer who may use channeling, cards, or horoscopes to alleviate a condition.

La familia. The family. Usually meant in reference to an extended family, complete with fictive kin.

Fé. Faith. An important factor in healing. Many Latinos have a strong faith in saints. The most revered is *La Virgen de Guadalupe*, the patron saint of the Americas.

Huesero. A lay bonesetter who sets simple fractures.

¡Si Dios quiere! If God wills it. A *dicho*. Expresses the belief that the ultimate fate of an enterprise is up to God, after humans have done all that they can. Should not be taken as a fatalistic statement.

Juramento. A vow or an oath. May be made to God or to a saint. The vow is usually accompanied by a monetary or physical sacrifice, which is undertaken to ensure a desired result. Can be used as a pledge to abstain from drinking.

Limpia. A cleansing. Folk healing method of removing the evil eye, performed by passing a branch of herbs or an egg over the body.

Macho. Masculine. In Latino culture, refers to manhood defined in terms of courage, independence, aggressiveness, or willingness to stand up to others in the most difficult and risky situations. The term can have negative connotations, describing a man who is, for example, capable of having multiple love affairs, or positive connotations, describing a man who is responsible, dignified, and bravely protects his family.

Mal de ojo. Evil eye. *Mal de ojo* may result from an envious relation between an adult and a child, or between two adults. Any illness that results from this type of influence requires a *limpia*, a cleansing ceremony practiced by a *curandera*, in which an egg is passed over the body, then opened and placed in a dish under the bed to absorb the bad spirits.

Misa. Mass. Attending Mass and receiving the Host may be perceived to provide healing powers.

Necio. Stubborn, difficult to get along with. May describe an individual whose behavior is inappropriate as the result of alcohol consumption.

Nervios. A common nonspecific complaint that may reflect anxiety or emotional instability. In Caribbean cultures, it may refer to a seizure disorder.

Partera. Midwife. In the hierarchy of healers, the one who is frequently in charge of the delivery of babies.

Pesado. Heavy. Used to describe an overbearing, nearly intolerable person.

Prender la vela. To light a votive candle, partly a religious act.

Sobadora. A healer, or *curandera*, who uses massage of the extremities or abdomen to relieve discomfort, including back pain, *empacho*, and pain arising from injuries.

Susto. A strong fright, an abrupt emotional shock resulting in a startling influence of long duration. May be perceived as causing the onset of chronic conditions such as diabetes or asthma.

Tamales (sing., *tamal*). A dish made of a filling surrounded by cornmeal paste that is steamed in corn husks or banana leaves. May be spicy or sweet.

Té de azahares. Tea made with orange or lemon blossoms. Used to treat insomnia in elderly patients. The remedy helps prevent addiction to sleeping pills.

Té de manzanilla. Chamomile tea. Sometimes referred to as the Mexican penicillin. One of the most common home remedies used in Latino folk medicine. Used to treat *empacho*. Can also be used as a cleansing agent for eye discharge related to conjunctivitis or for relief of hemorrhoids. Manzanilla leaves are also used as a poultice.

Té de orégano. Oregano tea. Used for relief of cough and congestion. May be added to a steam bath to open bronchial and nasal passages.

Tenedora. Birthing assistant who holds or supports women in labor.

Tú, solo tú. You, only you. The opening lines of a traditional Mexican song that tells of a man who drinks because a woman doesn't love him.

Uña de gato. Cat's claw. A much-promoted herbal product, prepared from the cortex of a tree in Latin America. Supposedly enhances the effectiveness of the neuro-logical apparatus in the fight against chronic diseases, including cancer and arthritis.

Velas. Candles. Lighting a candle has a spiritual effect that may result in healing.

Yerbero. A person with special knowledge of herbs and the use of herbal remedies.

Index